The
Singing Year

Candy Verney

Illustrated by Claudio Muñoz

Hawthorn Press

Published by Hawthorn Press, Hawthorn House,
1 Lansdown Lane, Stroud, Gloucestershire, GL5 1BJ, UK
Tel: (01453) 757040 Fax: (01453) 751138
Email: info@hawthornpress.com Website: **www.hawthornpress.com**

Drawings and cover illustration © Claudio Muñoz
Cover design and typesetting by Hawthorn Press, Stroud, Glos.
Additional illustrations by Sarah Fineran and Hawthorn Press
Printed by The Bath Press, Bath
Printed on environmentally friendly chlorine-free paper manufactured from renewable forest stock
CD recorded at DB Studios, Stroud, Glos.

Every effort has been made to trace the ownership of all copyrighted material and to acknowledge this. If any omission has been made, please bring this to the attention of the publisher so that proper acknowledgement can be made in future editions.

How far is it to Bethlehem, Frances Chesterton, by kind permission of A P Watt Ltd on behalf of The Royal Literary Fund. Autumn by Florence Hoatson by kind permission of Chambers Harrap Publishers Ltd. I am the wind, I breeze and blow, from *Pentatonic Songs,* by Elisabeth Lebret reprinted by kind permission of Waldorf Association of Ontario, The swing, Mary Osborn, My Wellington boots go, Rain, Lilian McCrea, Here we come a-haying, Eunice Close, Four scarlet berries, Mary Vivian, Over the dark water, The dandelion puff, from *Book of a Thousand Poems* reprinted by permission of HarperCollins Publishers Ltd. Pancake Tuesday, Hanukkah – One little candle, Hari Krishna, from *A Musical Calendar of Festivals,* Barbara Cass-Beggs, 1983 reprinted by permission of Ward Lock Educational. Shadows go round, Cotton field song, The winter now is over, Winter Night, The snowman, The Mitten Song, Lean daddy longlegs, Dilly duck, from *Sing through the Seasons,* Marlys Swinger, 1970 reprinted by kind permission of Plough Publishing House. The Tickle Rhyme, Anne Serraillier by kind permission of Jane Grossfeld. Snowdrop down, crocus up, by kind permission of Jean Lynch. Wake up, wake up all you little children, by kind permission of Jehanne Mehta. Hurry little children, come along with me, from *Singing and Dancing Games for the Very Young,* Esther L Nelson, 1982 Sterling Publishing Company. Celebrate Eid, Chinese New Year, Gung Hay Fat Choy, Nancy Stewart, Animal Crackers/Friends Street Music, 6505 SE 28th Street, Mercer Island, WA 98040, www.nancymusic.com.

British Library Cataloguing in Publication Data applied for

ISBN-10: 1 903458 39 0   ISBN-13: 978-1-903458-39-6

Contents

Acknowledgements

When I was first asked to write this book I knew that I wanted to draw on the experience of others; what did they remember of singing from their childhood and how significant a part did it play in bringing up their own children? I visited nursery schools and old peoples' day centres listening to the songs they sang and I sent out a circular letter to a wide variety of friends and colleagues asking for their contributions.

I had a wonderful response and I would like to thank everyone who contributed with songs, stories and memories. If I have missed anyone out from the list below, please accept my apologies.

I am left with a sense of awe at the deep impression music makes on the very young. It can be a marvellous tool to calm the hectic pace of modern family life and it remains an enduring memory and solace in old age.

There are not many traditional songs that lead us through the colours, smells and experiences of the seasons as seen through the eyes of a child. For this reason, when compiling *The Singing Year,* I decided to increase the existing repertoire myself. I was lucky enough to find two poets who agreed to create a series of seasonal poems which I then put music. This involved sending them lists of seasonal topics, for example, nettles, butterflies, grasshoppers, worms and snails (to name a few) for summer. A week or two later I would receive pages of poems that were touched with the rich sensual experience and magic of childhood – it felt a bit like 'sweetie day' for me! Some were so delightful as poems that I have left them as such. Others seemed to be made to sing, so I set them to music. I would like to offer sincere thanks and much appreciation to the poets Julie Tonkin and Nicola Wicksteed for their tireless work in collaborating with me over this book. Without their work, this book would be much the poorer.

I would also like to thank Rachel Jenkins and Martin Large of Hawthorn Press for originally asking me to write this book, and to my editor Matthew Barton for his patient and friendly support. And finally to my good friend Claudio Muñoz for enriching it with his beautiful illustrations.

Contributors

Aileen Taylor
Alison Hall
Amanda Relph
Anna Glasbrook
Annette Little
Brenda Davies
Bridget Holmes
Carolyn Pellow

Celia Bradshaw
Cindy Mann
Colin & Maggie Smith
Dr. Jean Brown
Elisabeth Marshall
Elizabeth Jackson
Ellen Matschke
Esther Lincoln

continued…

Eva Theophile
Hilary Martin
Jane Blackmoor
Jane Darlow
Jean Chancellor
Jean Lynch
Jenni Godwin
Jenny Drake
Jill Newsome
John & Ursula Brooke
Joy de Berker
Judith Verity
Julia Hyde Grossman
Julie Harding
Julie Hewson
Juliet Grainger
Juliet Harwood
Juliet Verney
Katerina Eisch
Ko Hawkes
Linda Webber
Lucy Gaskell
Lucy Metcalfe
Lyoba Jence
Margie Bickford-Smith
Margreth Pfunder-Sonn
Marion Green
Masami Cobley
Matilda Luetchford
Norma Middleton

Olu Oni
Patrick & Anna McCarron
Penny Willis
Peter Creed
Prue Musgrave
Rachel Campbell
Rebecca Reid
Rob Henley
Rose Verney
Sarah Davies
Sebastian Verney
Sheila Macbeth
Sonia Nicholson
Sue Dawkin
Sue Wade
Sulia Rose
Susan Amor
Susan Hicklin
Susan Lacroix
Suzanne Wise
Suzy Pritchard
Terence Molloy
Teresa Harris
Tricia McCleod
Ursula Mommins
Verona Bass
Vicki Knapp
Viv Cole
Viv Talbot

Foreword

Children love their seashell toys
And with them they learn about the ocean,
Because a little piece of the ocean
Inside the child, and inside the toy
Knows the whole ocean   Rumi *

The Singing Year recognizes the importance of nature's rhythms and of natural materials in children's development, and uses singing as a simple medium for sharing these gifts with young children, bringing rhythm, pattern, music and language into their lives. Just as Rumi's 'sea shell toys' contain a part of the whole ocean, so songs contain a key to a much wider world of language, pattern and time.

Whenever I go to the beach I am always amazed at the way children and adults quickly remember or 'relearn' how to play. The combination of nature's elements of water, rocks, sand, space and the rhythmic sound of the waves seem to awaken and stimulate our innate playfulness. From the most sophisticated urban executive parents, or the coolest teenagers, through to the 6-month-old baby who has just learned to sit, each can tap into a fundamental instinct to explore, experiment and create.

Recent research into young children's learning and development makes us increasingly aware of the importance of the early years (and even pre-birth in the womb) in creating the conditions for learning and development throughout life. Children are dynamic and powerful learners from the very beginning. The influence of their surroundings and their relationships with adults is crucial to physical brain development, as well as setting the context and foundations for physical and emotional wellbeing and lifelong learning. Children whose parents and carers sing and share music with them from birth, benefit significantly in terms of their ongoing development and learning.

If you are a parent you will find this book an invaluable resource to help develop your relationship with your child and your shared understanding of the wider world through daily singing that becomes an integral part of life. Many young children these days are cared for by other significant adults, sometimes for a large of part of each day. Relatives, childminders, nursery teachers, pre-school workers and family friends can all use singing to enhance what they offer, and to develop their relationships with children wherever they work or play.

Candy Verney has brought together a wonderful collection of simple songs, thoughtful insights and practical advice to help you develop and expand your repertoire. You don't even have to be able to sing well. Candy's advice for 'non-singers' and the CD provided to help you learn the songs will help. You may also want to share the book with other parents and carers so that you can learn the songs and develop confidence together.

I am delighted to recommend this book to you and wish you and the children in your care much joy in your singing.

Annie Davy
Head of Early Years and Childcare
Oxfordshire County Council –
Learning and Culture

---

*   from *Feeling the Shoulder of the Lion*, selected poetry and teaching stories from the Mathnawi, Threshold Books 1991

Dedication

To my beloved sons Henry, Ned and Theo,

who have taught me more than they realise

Introduction

I think that nursery rhymes are so deeply entrenched in our history that they speak to children. You cannot sing Twinkle, Twinkle Little Star, *or* Away in a Manger, *without the children loving it. You see their faces open up to that, and it obviously speaks far more deeply to them than we can ever imagine. I don't think we grownups have the consciousness left to realise how strong it is…*

What singing means to me

I have always loved songs. From my teenage years onwards I found myself collecting ditties, folk songs and skipping games whenever they came my way. But it was not until I had children of my own that I realised their practical potential. Lullabies – what a lovely, lulling word – soon showed me they held the magical power to soothe a crying child to sleep.

When my first child was born I would anxiously get up in the night so that he did not have to cry for more than a few seconds. Feeding him and trying to get him back to sleep exhausted me. For my third baby, a friend lent me a cradle with a stand which swung on hinges. Suddenly, all I had to do was lean, half asleep, out of my bed, rock the cradle, and the baby would drop off to sleep again. The rhythm of the rocking did the job for me. Why hadn't someone told me about this sooner I wondered? Why did cradles ever go out of fashion? So simple – just the rhythm of rocking calmed the child.

A few years later, one winter's evening, bedtime for my three children, all under five years old, was long overdue. But they were wound up like cars on a racetrack. The higher the emotional temperature rose, the more tired they became. I felt close to breaking point, about to lose my temper, when I remembered a game that my father used to play with us around the dinner table. He would sit in the space between the table and the wall, swinging his arm rhythmically, side to side, as we children ran around the table, taking turns to get through the gap without his arm touching us. I still remember the beating of my heart and my excitement: would I get caught, would I get through? Then the moment of enlightenment when I realised that I could slip past by keeping in time with the rhythm of his arm. I never got caught again!

On that damp November evening, as a creative alternative to losing my temper and spoiling our evening, it came into my mind to try this game, and see if it would calm them down. Spontaneously, I put the movement to a little rhyme, sung to the tune of *The Grand Old Duke of York*:

> *O a-hunting we will go*
> *Across the fields of snow*
> *We'll catch a fox and put him in the box*
> *And then we'll let him go*

I sat on a child's seat in their bedroom and swung my arm to and fro in the gap between my chair and the bunk beds. As if by magic, the children joined in the game. Each time I caught one of them, I took off a piece of their clothing. Before long, to my amazement, they were tucked up in bed, ready for a story, without trouble or conflict; the job of undressing had been transformed from a chore to a much-loved game that we continued to play for years. In fact, when I recently asked my sixteen-year-old son if he remembered any songs from his childhood, his face lit up immediately. 'Yes, you know, that fox one!'

Song builds up inner resources in children. The lifelong value of this was brought home to me as I researched this book. In the process of collecting songs I have received replies from people up to the age of ninety, who remember the songs sung to them when they were very little children: not only the tunes, but all the verses as well. They were given a treasure chest as children that has served them for the rest of their lives, into which they can dip at any time. One old lady, now nearly blind, deaf, and immobilised, responded when I commiserated with her: 'Oh, I can lie here and recite all my poems to myself.' She has retained an immense repertoire of poetry, first taught to her as a child in Ireland.

Sadly, many of us today have been brought up with very few rhymes, poems or songs. Singing as part of family life is rare – even singing in schools can no longer be taken for granted. But children only need to hear the smallest ditty twice for them to eagerly ask for it again, encouraging you to sing to them. They imitate as easily as breathing. They will readily join in, helping to fill their own inner treasure chest.

As a child, journeys to the seaside with my family seemed endlessly long. We often sang the well-known Harry Belafonte song, *There's a hole in my bucket, dear Lisa, dear Lisa* in which my father would take the lead with obvious pleasure. It wasn't often that we heard him sing, and it managed to break the monotony of that tedious journey. I've liked that song ever since.

My mother would sing arias from her favourite operas around the house. As self-conscious teenagers we teased her about this habit, but with hindsight it gave us all a life-long love of music. She also had a way of reading nursery rhymes and little children's stories, slowly and rhythmically, yet with music and playfulness in her voice. The sing-song rhythm had a soothing effect on me. I found it immediately reassuring, as if we were both cocooned in a dream world that for a few minutes replaced everyday reality.

A parental resource

Singing can be of immense help to parents in the long haul of everyday routine. It lightens the atmosphere between grownup and child, can transform a situation from drudgery into playfulness, and also ease the transition from one activity to the next. *Whatever you feel about the quality of your voice, the most important thing from the child's point of view is that you sing.* (See below for help with developing more confidence in singing.) You should feel free to make up your own version of a song to suit each occasion. Nursery songs are part of a wise and generous folk tradition, a body of literature and tunes that expands organically and evolves to suit each generation.

Singing and the natural world

This companion volume to *The Singing Day* focuses on our annual journey through the seasons. In days gone by, and still today in more traditional cultures, children absorbed nature's rhythms and laws through their daily lives. They saw people around them growing food, weaving clothes from wool or cotton, building houses from the locally available materials. They directly experienced the relationship between themselves and nature.

However, with the vast majority of people in the western world living in urban environments, it is usual for children to grow up unaware of this relationship. Singing, along with stories, can play a major role in bringing to life our traditional connection and dependence on the natural world, within a language that children understand. Young children learn through doing. When a child sings about chopping wood, and performs the movements that are involved, or crouches under a blanket, being a little seed under the ground waiting to come up in spring, she* is absorbing these natural relationships into her growing body: the cycles of nature, the seasons, the source of our food, a respect for animals. This fundamental truth has, alas, sometimes been dismissed as romantic, but however sophisticated we become, our food is still grown in spring, needs the rain and the sun to ripen, and is harvested in autumn. The child who has built these connections inside herself will not only become more 'grounded' psychologically, but will live her adult life with these connections in mind, and with an innate awareness of her natural surroundings.

Seasonal activities

Growing plants with children, or having them in the garden where they can touch, smell and feel them, watch their annual cycle from new bud to blossom, then to fruit and autumnal decay, fosters a relationship with nature and therefore with the greater rhythmic cycles of the year.

It is easy for children nowadays to grow up having little opportunity to develop and refine their senses. They are bombarded with noise and visual TV images, but what about the subtler impressions: the smell of damp leaves in a wood, the exquisite unfolding of a fern in spring, or the sight of a bee making its rounds of the open cupped summer flowers? Many children's play areas have little in them except grass. In his 'Centuries of Meditations' written in the seventeenth century, Thomas Traherne vividly describes the intensity of childhood impressions:

The corn was orient and immortal wheat, which never should be reaped, nor was ever sown. I thought it had stood from everlasting to ever-lasting. The dust and stones of the street were as precious as gold: the gates were at first the end of the world. The green trees when I saw them first through one of the gates transported me and ravished me, their sweetness and unusual beauty made my heart to leap, and almost mad with ecstasy, they were strange and wonderful things.

With these thoughts in mind, I have included lists of plants that are easily grown. Each has something about them that appeals to children whether it be the shape, the smell, the sound of their name, or their use in play. I have also included simple activities that encourage this interaction, and many have accompanying songs.

Singing and our global community

As well as rooting a child within his own culture, singing also has a valuable part to play in fostering an appreciation of other cultures and awakening children to the wider human world, to its diversity and richness. Here is a song that was taught to me when I was a little girl:

The little German girl goes Eins, zwei, drei..
The little French girl goes Un, deux, trois…

I was intrigued to think that there were children in other places who said those strange words! Singing a song can open a window into that other culture. With this in

---

*   To avoid the awkward use of 'he or she', I will alternate between masculine and feminine forms

mind, I have included a few songs in other languages.

Likewise, when a child is involved in a ring game, he is partaking of an activity that has gone on throughout the world since ancient times. The themes of courtship, marriage, war and celebration represent archetypal human activities. By dancing and singing together, we connect to what is universal, and we are reaffirming our union in a common humanity and our place on this unique planet.

The practice of music is our legacy and heritage – perhaps the oldest and most sacred of our musical traditions. Born of an awareness that in some way music-making made us feel bolder and less afraid, music was a vehicle through which we expressed the interconnectedness of our pulsing universe and the unity of its rhythmic cycles long before we were able to give verbal expression to the concepts that were beginning to take shape in our minds. And in that experience of union is music's primary value as a healing force. Overcoming the anxiety of separateness in a world so often perceived as hostile, music is the reassurance of the harmony and purposefulness, the essential order and beneficence of the universe.
RANDALL MCCLELLAN
Healing Forces of Music

Singing with children in the early years

All appeared new, and strange at first, inexpressibly rare and delightful and beautiful. I was a little stranger, which at my entrance into the world was saluted and surrounded with innumerable joys. My knowledge was Divine…
THOMAS TRAHERNE

There are so many reasons for singing with children from the very beginning of their lives (this book focuses particularly on the first three or four years). Above all, they delight in it. They will dance and sing spontaneously when they are happy – a sure sign of their wellbeing. This was brought home to me clearly once when some neighbours of mine, experienced foster parents, adopted three little sisters. On a visit to their household a few months after the children had arrived, I saw the four-year-old meandering around the garden, in her own world, singing away to herself, clearly showing she had settled into her new home and was happy.

Besides pure joy in singing, there are also developmental and educational reasons which make singing an essential activity in these early years.

Singing development in infants

From their earliest beginnings inside the womb, babies respond to music. As early as three months they start moving to music, rhythmically swaying or bouncing. The existence of games for babies throughout the world – foot play, finger play, Peek-a-boo – are testimony to children's love of and need for such structured movement.

Toddlers will dance as soon as they can stand up. At about eight months, after the babbling stage, their first songs are often wonderfully inventive, using snatches of songs they have heard and mixing them with their own repertoire of words and phrases. Psychologists call these 'outline songs'. Though they are not exact imitations of known songs, they follow the gist or the contour of a song. This is a form of dreamy musical play, and a necessary stage of development in preparation for other forms of music making. These early experimentations represent children's self-activity, the roots of their lifelong creativity. They are mastering their native music, making it their own, and expressing their own inner state at the same time.

Parents and primary carers naturally talk to their infants from birth in a way particularly suited to their child. Psychologists have called this verbal interaction 'motherese'. Often the infant initiates this and the adult responds. This form of communication between adult and infant exists universally across cultures and plays a major role in babies' speech and singing development. It is amazing that mothers throughout the world use similar or identical melodic phrases to communicate similar emotions such as approval, warning, soothing and love.

From my experience of remedial work with adults unable to hold a melody when singing, I believe that 'non-singers' had no one in their early years who sang and spoke 'motherese' to them. As a result their voices never learnt to imitate tunes, to 'fine-tune' themselves. Singing to children helps the voice find and orientate itself, helps voice and ear co-operate in reproducing a tune.

It is important not to censor, correct or hurry these early stages. Children vary enormously in their capacity and speed when learning to sing 'in tune' as adults would define it. Some sing beautifully before they are one, others only learn at eight or nine, and then only if given some help with conscious listening. It does not mean they are 'unmusical', and real damage may be done to both voice and self-esteem if corrections are made too early, or in a critical manner.

My early experiences of singing were that my mother had perfect pitch; so if I sang she would correct the notes and tell me that I was doing it wrong. As a result, I have always felt that I couldn't sing.

It is worth noting that our judgement of what is 'in tune' or not is culturally specific. The underlying scale (or series of notes) we use in the modern western world is only one of many that have developed in other cultures over the centuries. What sounds in tune for us will sound out of tune to others around the world, whose music is based on a different tuning system. Our western contemporary tuning (for instance on the piano) is a contrivance that came into use in the eighteenth century, when some intervals were compressed to make them fit into a system, so-called equal temperament. While most adults have learnt to sing these intervals, the small child will not, because her organ of hearing has not yet adapted to our cultural confines.

Singing and movement as aids to other learning

In addition to purely musical development, singing and movement are central to many other areas of children's learning. Piaget first identified the time between 0-3 years as the 'sensory-motor' stage of development, meaning that sensation and movement are the primary way in which children learn about themselves and their environment. Children at this age need to run, jump, skip, tumble, roll and be vocal. They are co-ordinating their muscles, learning about balance, training their memories, which they need to do sufficiently before they can be asked to sit still and learn in a conventional way.*

In the field of memory, a child learns the skills of reading, writing, spelling and counting after

---

* See book by Sally Goddard Blythe listed in the Bibliography

first developing three basic memory skills: visio-spatial, auditory and short-term memory. Music and movement are intrinsic to developing all three. Visio-spatial skill grows out of the child's knowledge of himself in space, through balancing and movement; auditory memory develops through listening, speaking and singing; and short term memory develops through repetition. As regards word-building, Sally Goddard Blythe, from the Institute of Neurophysiological Psychology, Chester, has done extensive research in this field, and describes music as one of the most powerful instruments we have to give children a basic reference library of sounds.★ A list of other recent studies corroborating these findings are listed in the Bibliography.

One of the greatest music educators of the twentieth century, Zoltan Kodaly, spent a major part of his life researching and promoting the benefits children gain from singing. As a result of his work, the Hungarian government set up a series of music primary schools all over Hungary from 1950 onwards, which were open to children regardless of musical ability. Here, singing

---

★ In *Music and Movement,* p7, she writes:

The process of vocalising sounds to music builds up a storehouse of vocabulary, or lexicon, which may be called upon at any time. The process of putting words to music, and of pointing, naturally breaks words down into separate syllables by giving one or several notes for each unit of sound within the word, placing emphasis on key consonants and slowing down the sounds of speech, so that every phoneme within a word is articulated. In this way, not only is the voice trained, but also the ear, the eye and memory.

and music were part of the daily curriculum. The educational development of children from these schools was compared over a number of years with those in normal state primary schools. The results were dramatic. In addition to an expected increase in musical ability, those in the music primary schools demonstrated a vastly increased capacity in other educational areas:

- ability to memorise
- capacity for reasoning and disciplined thinking
- richness of emotional range in descriptive writing and speaking
- more active participation in school work
- increased ability to learn foreign languages, through better capacity to imitate, concentrate and memorise
- aesthetic awareness and sensitivity to colour, expressed in a greater facility for drawing and painting
- improved development of children's thorax and respiratory organs, and likewise their awareness of breathing

From my own work in primary schools I can corroborate these findings. In a school where music and movement had been deleted from the curriculum for at least two years, due to pressure to improve literacy and numeracy, the children had difficulty moving fluidly, their movements were uncoordinated and awkward, their singing voices largely out of tune, and most children could not stamp or clap in time. The image that came to me as I sang and moved with the children was of pouring water on dry, parched earth.

Kodaly advised that if a child is having difficulty learning the 3 Rs, one should give him more time for singing and movement, and this would help with academic learning.

A word about rhythm and repetition

Children live in the heart of the ocean of time itself, in an everlasting now. A child's eternal present is present-absorbed, present-spontaneous, present-elastic.

JAY GRIFFITHS,
Pip Pip, A Sideways Look at Time

Rhythm is very important in young children's lives. Not so much the mechanical beat of the metronome, but the movement of the breath, contraction and expansion like the sea's tide flowing in and out. Children have no use for, and no conception of linear time, but they thrive when their day has a breathing rhythm, a flow between the IN of peace, rest, reflection; and the OUT of activity, action and interest in the world.

When such rhythm becomes a part of the child's everyday experience, it promotes health and contentment, and strengthens growing life forces. The world is chaotic without rhythm. Singing can be used as signposts and cornerstones to mark these flowing rhythms: not only of the day, but also the longer rhythms of the week, and to celebrate the annual rhythms of the seasons and the cycle of the year.

A repertoire of songs repeatedly sung at 'tidy up time', or at bedtime, can foster a child's sense of security and build self-confidence. As she grows older, so songs may change to suit differing needs. But some will remain as family favourites.

Rhythm can also enter the way we actually sing songs to little ones. With young children we do not aim for a precise, metronome rhythm that would fit with a drumbeat, but one that reflects a song's words and mood. Sing it liltingly, feeling free to slow down to anticipate some action, speeding up again to reflect the meaning of the words. This is enlivening to young children, as their response will prove.

Here are the observations of two nursery teachers, relating how rhythm helps them in their daily work with children:

Singing to children brings about that transparent quality in them; they're so open to song, and they'll look at you with their shining eyes. We use so much instruction, so much spoken word. But you can use singing to do all the chivvying along, and they will always respond to it so well. In the nursery, a song will be an indication that something's starting or something's ending. It makes transitions so much easier. Children live in a musical element, they live in the music.

Many children today are in situations where they are prematurely woken to a wider world, with its adult preoccupations, expectations and dangers… Their inborn trust is frequently shaken by the inconsistencies in their lives: Is Daddy leaving? Who will pick me up? Where are we going now? … Anxieties can and do gradually ease, however, as the kindergarten's daily and weekly rhythms lift from the child the burden of wondering what will come next, what will be expected of her. The steady, returning rhythms of the kindergarten are particularly healing for children in difficult circumstances. They signal to the child: "Here you are safe and you can trust in what you'll find." *

What sort of music?

It is worth giving some thought to the kind of music that we use with young children. Obviously there is tremendous value in nursery rhymes and well-known songs, some of which are included in this collection.

---

* Lynne Oldfield in *Free to Learn*

When introducing new songs it is also worth bearing in mind that the pentatonic scale is particularly suited to young children.

D   E   G   A   B

If a child first has a firm grasp of the five 'pillar' tones of the pentatonic scale, he will later find it easy to fit in the half step between them.

KATALIN FORRAI
Music in Preschool

This is a scale found in folk music all over the world, and from the most ancient times. Parts of it are used instinctively by children in their games, as in the phrases 'I'm the king of the castle', and 'I'm coming, ready or not'. It has an innate simplicity, with no semitones in the scale, which makes it easier to sing. It also can float naturally here and there, without a strong pull down to the 'home' note, the tonic, as in our major and minor scales. This reflects where young children are at, in a consciousness of imaginative make-believe, in a world which is dreamy and not yet anchored in more mundane realities or focused tasks.

Many of the seasonal songs included in this book are pentatonic. They may sound unfamiliar at first hearing. This is because our adult ears have become conditioned to hearing a predominance of music in major and minor keys. But young children are very happy with them.

A word about recorded versus live music

Although tapes and CDs have their place, there is nothing that equals the value of a child's very own 'live music': that of being sung to. We accept that physical nourishment is vital for the child's growing body, but are less likely to recognise that everything else the child takes in through his senses has a similar effect. Just as children need and thrive on human touch, human response and love, so they need to hear the sound of the human voice. Voice production is a highly complex and finely tuned process. Children need to make complex observations, trials, experiments with their voice, that are learnt from the people around them. It is the direct connection that is important: when a mother sings to her baby, she transmits a range of tones, frequencies, breathing patterns, facial movements and vitality that is impossible to replicate in a tape or CD.

A word of warning

Infants have highly sensitive ears that can be damaged, literally 'de-tuned', by very loud or low frequency sounds. Exposure to loud sounds over extended periods of time will prompt the ear to tune out certain frequencies to protect itself, and as a result, will be less able to listen and learn well. For further reading on this issue, I recommend the work of Dr. Alfred Tomatis (see Bibliography), who has connected auditory damage to many chronic conditions e.g. dyslexia, depression, Attention Deficit Disorder (ADD), and Hyperactivity (ADHD).

Incorporating songs into everyday life

The fact delighted in is the special performance for the strictly limited audience. A mother's own voice is worth more than four-and-twenty professional singers trilling on the radio.

OPIE AND OPIE
Oxford Nursery Rhyme Book

So where do we start? A natural place would be to sing the very familiar nursery rhymes that you probably know from your own childhood:

- Round and round the garden like a teddy bear
- Here we go round the mulberry bush
- Humpty Dumpty

etc.

You will find that they flow easily: part of your own store of memories.

The wonderful thing about singing at home is that there is no right and wrong way to do it, no copyright laws to worry about, no experts to advise you – you can develop your own personal family repertoire, singing the songs that develop between individual members of your family. It is a wonderful way to nurture family closeness, to develop a shared history, your own family's treasure chest. Singing establishes confidence and a sense of security.

I watch children who haven't had singing in their lives before: they look at you and stare and giggle, they love it so much. They get such joy from it. The repetition in songs is really important as well.

SARAH DAVIES
Nursery Teacher

Accompaniments

Although some song books have piano/guitar accompaniment, and children will enjoy singing along when someone is playing an instrument, the most important thing for younger ones is the direct connection between you and them, not only your attention, but the physical movements that spontaneously happen when you sing with them – the rocking, jiggling, clapping and games.

'Of course I can't make up my own songs...'

Well, yes, of course you can! The spontaneous act of making up a story or song with or for a child is a precious gift to him. High poetry is not needed, but just that attention to the child and creativity in response to him, which he senses directly. My father used to make up stories for us as children. They centred on a character called Little Mo. I have forgotten the storyline, but I still remember the joy and inner glow that I felt when he related another episode.

You can start with a well known tune like *Here we go round the mulberry bush* and make up the simplest of ditties that express some activity that you do regularly with your child: getting undressed, going upstairs, putting on coats and hats. The child will especially love it if his own name is included. Here are three very simple examples:

This is the way we water the garden,
water the garden, water the garden etc.
(to the tune of *Mulberry Bush*)

Oh the shopping trolley is full,
we'll have to give it a pull.
(*Grand Old Duke of York*)

'Joey's feet are climbing up,
One, two, one, two,
We're going up the stairs,
Till we reach the top!'
(Sung rhythmically, in time with your steps)

Children not only appreciate your efforts, however timid, but they will copy you, and probably outstrip you in humour and quality. I asked the mothers of children who had been coming to a toddler singing group for several months what effect the singing had on their children, and whether it affected their family life. Here are some responses:

We were going round a supermarket. Emily was bored, she started singing, making up her own words to familiar tunes about what she could see – e.g. putting the pasta in the basket. When we're out and about, people comment on how happy she seems, as she's always singing to herself.

Maisie was full of excitement in the car one morning, as she had seen a baby lamb on the way. I expressed interest in what she had seen. Then she suddenly said, 'Sing it!' She is used to singing her way through life.

Our singing toddlers' group has increased my confidence and stopped me feeling inhibited about singing. It's just part of normal life now. It has given us another easily accessible tool, another strand to my daughter's and my relationship. It's very much around.

When Emily, aged 2¹/₂, doesn't want to do something, or I find we need to change activity, I start singing it, e.g. 'We're all going to the shops.' She then becomes keen to do it.

When Isaac was younger and could not yet talk, he used some of the songs and their actions to communicate. For example he would tell me to stop by bringing his arms down and slapping his knees, an action we had done in the rhyme Roly Poly.

Lily (just 2 years) doesn't sing that much yet, but she recognises all the songs.

'I love music, but I can't sing' – encouragement for reticent singers

Many people describe themselves as being unable to sing. This is an effect of our modern life style. Unless we were very lucky, we did not experience much singing in our childhood. As a result, we never developed the habit, our voices did not get a chance to learn, and our innate confidence drained away.

In former days, as we have seen, singing was a daily activity that accompanied the rhythms of work, whether hammering on an anvil, washing clothes, or pulling in the nets, as well as being a central activity in community entertainment. Children were brought up hearing the adults around them singing, and consequently learned to sing. There are many places in the world where singing still plays a daily part in the celebration of life.

Many 'non-singers' can remember an incident in their childhood when a teacher, a parent or another child made a critical comment about their voice which humiliated them. From then on, sometimes for a lifetime, they have kept quiet. Damaging comments of this kind often come from a misguided belief that singing is a gift you are or are not born with. Children are either 'musical' or not. Even today, in schools, most children are not taught to sing. It is a curious anomaly that we expect to teach children to read and write, but think they should be able to sing without help.

The following comments are by adults who learned how to sing in midlife, and continue to gain immense pleasure from it:

It was just before Christmas and I was 6½ years old. The infants' choir for the nativity play had been chosen. I was not in it but not everyone was. Another of the infants' teachers then selected a non-choir group to go around the classes singing carols outside the classroom doors. I was the only non-choir member not selected. This is when I knew I could not sing.

SA

As a child I didn't sing; we didn't sing at home and I don't remember singing at school. My parents were always too busy to sing and I grew up with a belief that I was tone deaf, frightened to utter a note in case it was the wrong one. I have always lacked confidence in expressing myself.

In my work I find that most 'non-singers' *can* sing – they can sing in tune and have a sense of rhythm. But they lack confidence. Our feelings of inhibition and embarrassment at singing in company get passed on to our children, and this eventually curtails their natural and spontaneous love of singing and dancing. The wonderful thing is that our young children's delight in these activities and their innate tolerance and trust of us can help us reverse this negative cycle. We only have to try a little, and their enthusiasm will encourage us. Once we have got over initial embarrassment, the child's positive responses will help.

It is also useful to know that there are a number of steps we can take to restore our voice to its natural capacity.

There are two main areas to look at – breathing and listening.

Breathing

In a natural and healthy breathing system the body is a relaxed organism, the breath flowing in deeply to the abdomen, then out again. This continues as we sing. Those who feel they cannot copy a tune probably experienced a time in their childhood when a part of their singing apparatus was blocked in some way. Tensions and constrictions can build up in any one of several areas of the body used in singing: the head, neck and throat, shoulders, chest and abdomen.

Breathing exercise

The Avon Gorge in Bristol is a deep muddy ravine, with the river Avon flowing through it. This immense body of water flows in and out twice a day, rising 30 feet from high to low tide. But the riverbed that contains all the water does not move at all.

Imagine your body is the riverbed, and the air you breathe is its tidal water. Lie on your back, head supported and raised a little, so that all your vertebrae are flat on the floor. Raise the knees, hands resting on the stomach, get really comfortable, and breathe normally. Imagine yourself as the river gorge, lying still and relaxed, and your breath like the water flowing in through an open channel, then flowing out again, out, out, out... so that the tide is out completely, there is no water left in the river bed. Just as the gorge does not *actively* suck the water back, so you *allow* the breath to flow back in by itself, feel yourself opening up, there is no effort involved, until the river is high again. Aim for a state of peace and relaxation. Only the belly gently swells as the breath comes in, and then flattens as the breath goes out – the shoulders, neck and throat should remain relaxed, hardly moving.

Then slowly stand up, keeping the same state of relaxation, shoulders relaxed, no tension in the chest or neck as the breath flows in and out. Now try humming, chanting any note. If this comes easily, try singing a few notes, maybe with someone you trust. If you can maintain this relaxed and natural breathing state and sing at the same time, you are well on the way to finding your voice.

Listening

There is a difference between hearing and listening. As I sit here at the computer my son is listening to the radio; it is a glorious spring day and the birds are singing outside. For most of the morning I have not heard the birds or the radio. I have been absorbed in my own thought process, writing these words. But the sounds are still travelling along my auditory nerves to my brain. It is my perceptual awareness that changes, enabling me either to listen or not. If I pause from my work, I can start listening, and the birds and radio will come into my hearing again.

The background level of noise in our urban world does not encourage us to listen. We hear all the sounds around us, but the ear learns to cut off, to protect itself from over-stimulation.

In fact we can improve our singing voice by learning to listen. People who feel unconfident when singing often hear the note, then panic at the thought of having to reproduce it. They rush to sing, as if the speed will somehow get the ordeal over with quickly. But their ears may not have had a chance to listen to the note.

Listening exercises

Work with a trusted friend or teacher.

1. She sings a note.
   You breathe out strongly, then breathe in and try to sing the same note.
   Repeat with the same or other notes, establishing a rhythm between you.

2. She sings a note
   Listen to the note first, *pause,* sing the note inside your head, then try to reproduce it.

3. Singing while moving is also very helpful. Panic is linked to thoughts. If you move while singing the thought process is kept at bay, so that the natural voice has a chance to come out. Pretend to dig up potatoes as you sing; or march, jump or swing your arms.

As you concentrate on improving your singing voice in these ways – through breathing and listening – your hearing will become more acute. You may start to hear subtleties in sounds that you were unaware of before, e.g. whether a note is higher or lower than its neighbour.

Starting to sing

However you feel about your voice, just try starting with a simple song, maybe a very simple one, e.g. *Little red robin* (page 18). Learn it off by heart, then sing it to your child.

After two or three times your child will start responding, showing recognition, which will encourage you to carry on. You may find the child is delighted!

If you really feel you cannot keep a tune at all, then try speaking or chanting a rhyme to accompany an activity, e.g. *A little bit of blowing* (page 4) when you see some spring bulbs starting to grow in the park or garden, or *Around we go, around we go, a-whirling in the wind* (page 75) accompanied by the actions. The child's obvious enjoyment will soon encourage you.

Build up a few rhymes that you and your child enjoy. This will develop your confidence.

Then ask a trusted friend to sing a very simple song with you. You could start with the two notes of the cuckoo's song, 'Cuckoo!' Sing it over and over again, making sure that they always start on the same note. If that goes well, add an extra note so that you are singing the notes of

> 'I'm the king of the castle
> Get down you dirty rascal'

Now you could try some of the songs in this book:
Pebbles (page 55)
Busy bee (page 39)
I am the wind (page 74)
Little red robin (page 18)
Rabbit (page 95)

One woman, Sulia, found it hard to pitch notes or to sing high. She recognised a joy for singing in her eldest child and wanted her children not to be blocked as she had been. So she came for singing lessons, and made a tape of songs for them all to learn, herself included. It developed her confidence, and also helped her children learn to sing from her, their dad and the tape. They learned through her enthusiasm and perseverance

– and began to tell her when she was out of tune! The children now all sing beautifully and it is a major part of their family life. There are professional teachers who specialise in helping people find their voice (see 'Organisations' at back of book). Before you sign up for a lesson, check that they work with 'non-singers'. I have never met anyone who could not learn to sing with help. Nor have I met anyone who was 'tone deaf'. See Natural Voice Practitioners' Network to find a teacher.

Helping children sing

Below are some teaching techniques that help children to tune their voices and sing well at a young age:

- Try to start on the same note each time you repeat a song. This is comparable to giving the voice a map to orient itself.
- Sing quite high – children's voices are naturally higher than adults.
- Repetition: children love and need to have songs repeated. I sing each song two or three times at a go, especially when I have just introduced it. Then I continue to sing it for many consecutive sessions. Not only do children love the familiarity they gain in this way, but it helps to tune their voices. I gradually introduce other songs and drop the original ones, keeping a balance between familiarity and new interest.
- Sing at a pace that suits the age of the child. Don't sing too fast. Children need time to grasp tunes and accompanying actions.
- Be flexible with the rhythm. I often pause on the first note of a song. This indicates to the children that we are starting, and 'gathers them in'. It also helps their voices

to find the note (even adults need this), and brings a playful feeling of anticipation to the music.

- Movement is central to helping children sing in tune and find the rhythm. You can help a child by holding his hand and walking along, singing the song in time with your feet, or bouncing him gently on your knee.
- Children pick up the mood you create. Be playful, enjoy yourself!

And a few final notes...

Finally, a note about the selection of songs: I have included a few very well known nursery songs, but there are many I have left out, for the simple reason that they are readily available elsewhere.

You will notice that when the songs are sung on CD, the singer does not follow the exact rhythm of the notes. This is done deliberately. Bar lines in written music are limiting and mechanical (see section on rhythm): they cannot possibly show all the nuances of music that is alive and fresh. It is this fresh quality which feeds the young child's heart and soul, so don't curtail your natural talents by sticking too rigidly to beat or bar lines. You are in good company – Chopin did it all the time!

Singing rounds

Young children are not likely to be able to hold a tune 'against' others as is necessary in a round. But they can still enjoy the sounds of the harmonies if older children and adults sing rounds.

Spring

The vast treasure house of song around the seasons and
festivals is the soil and sun and air and light of the garden of
childhood, with its green hills and dark, fretful corners.

ROB HENLEY

Early Spring

Snowdrop down

CD TRACK 1

WORDS: JEAN LYNCH   MUSIC: CANDY VERNEY

Snowdrop down,   crocus   up   Head held down, and   head held   up,

Down to Mother Earth And up to Father Sun   Winter is   over,   and spring has begun.

Snowdrop down, crocus up   *(make bud shape with hands, point down, point up)*
Head held down, and head held up,   *(repeat)*
Down to Mother Earth   *(point arms down)*
And up to Father Sun   *(point arms up)*
Winter is over, and spring has begun.   *(hands by cheek, 'asleep', jump, or hold hands and dance)*

*Every time we found a bunch of snowdrops,
my children would of their own accord, sing
a snowdrop song.*

I found a tiny snowdrop
A-blooming in the cold.
I'll share with you a secret
The little flower told.
Though winter still is here
He hasn't long to stay,
I came across to tell you
That spring is on its way.
                    CHRISTINA T. OWEN

In my oaken mossy root
I will hold you clear and bright
I will watch you bend your head
Snowy snowdrops green and white

In among my woody claws
I will hold you clear and bright
I will watch you sway your leaf
Snowy snowdrops green and white
                    JULIE TONKIN

Snow white, white snow, *(spread arms out horizontally, hands facing up, then facing down)*
Heaven above and earth below *(arms stretched up, then down)*
Spring come, winter go, *(beckon with one hand, wave with the other)*
Snowdrop. *(cup hands, like snowdrop)*   ANON.

Spring Gone Shy

CD TRACK 2

WORDS: NICOLA WICKSTEED   MUSIC: CANDY VERNEY

It's supposed to be spring, but spring has gone all shy;

That's because King Winter doesn't want to say, 'Goodbye'. Just as the daff-o-dils be-

gan to make a show, back came King Winter With a blast of ice and snow.

It's supposed to be spring,
But spring has gone all shy;
That's because King Winter
Doesn't want to say, 'Goodbye'.
Just as the daffodils
Began to make a show,
Back came King Winter
With a blast of ice and snow.

A little bit of blowing
A little bit of snowing
A little bit of growing
And the crocuses will show.
                    ANON.

Waiting for Leaves

CD TRACK 3

WORDS: NICOLA WICKSTEED   MUSIC: CANDY VERNEY

The snowdrops are out and the crocuses are out. The daffodils are nearly there, but the new spring leaves can't be seen on the trees, the branches of the trees look bare.

The snowdrops are out
And the crocuses are out.
The daffodils are nearly there,
But the new spring leaves
Can't be seen on the trees,
The branches of the trees look bare.

The snowdrops are out
And the crocuses are out.
The daffodils are nearly there,
When the buds on the trees
Open out into leaves,
No longer will the trees look bare.

Crocus, crocus waken up, *(arms above head, pointed up)*
To catch a sunbeam in your cup. *(open arms wide)*

ANON.

Wake up, all you little children

CD TRACK 4

WORDS AND MUSIC: J. MEHTA

Wake up, wake up, all you little children, sunlight, sky bright, spring is coming now.

Gusty March winds blowing, daffodils a- growing, birds sing, bells ring. There's blossom on the bough.

Wake up, wake up, all you little children,
Sunlight, sky bright, spring is coming now.
Gusty March winds blowing, daffodils a-growing,
Birds sing, bells ring. There's blossom on the bough.

The Seed

Baby seedlings in the earth below
Wait for Sun and Rain to make them grow.
When Spring arrives, down go their roots
And up into the air pops new fresh shoots.

NICOLA WICKSTEED

Daffydown dilly is new come to town
With a yellow petticoat
And a green gown.

TRADITIONAL

6

Wake up!

CD TRACK 5

WORDS: NICOLA WICKSTEED   MUSIC: CANDY VERNEY

I'm a dormouse; I've slept the winter through. Curled up in my nest, I've slept the winter through.

Come the springtime   This is what I do: WAKE UP!   Scrabble scrabble here

Scrabble scrabble there, looking for my food, scrabble scrabble scrabble scrabble everywhere!

I'm a dormouse;
I've slept the winter through.
Curled up in my nest,
I've slept the winter through.
Come the springtime
This is what I do:

WAKE UP! Scrabble scrabble here
Scrabble scrabble there, looking for my food,
Scrabble scrabble scrabble scrabble
Everywhere!

I'm a green frog;
I've slept the winter through.
Underneath the mud,
I've slept the winter through.
Come the springtime
This is what I do:

WAKE UP! Jumping jumping here
Jumping jumping there, looking for my food,
Jumping jumping jumping jumping
Everywhere!

I'm a grass snake;
I've slept the winter through.
In a compost heap,
I've slept the winter through.
Come the springtime
This is what I do:

WAKE UP! Slither slither here
Slither slither there, looking for my food,
Slither slither slither slither
Everywhere!

I'm a small bat;
I've slept the winter through.
Hanging in a barn,
I've slept the winter through.
Come the springtime
This is what I do:

WAKE UP! Flitter flitter here
Flitter flitter there, looking for my food,
Flitter flitter flitter flitter
Everywhere!

Catkins

CD TRACK 6

WORDS: NICOLA WICKSTEED

MUSIC: CANDY VERNEY

I love catkins, delicate catkins, but why are they catkins not dogkins or ratkins?

Why are they catkins not dogkins or rat-kins, those dancing, dangling, delicate catkins?

I love catkins,
Delicate catkins,
But why are they catkins
Not dogkins or ratkins?
Why are they catkins
Not dogkins or ratkins,
Those dancing, dangling,
Delicate catkins?

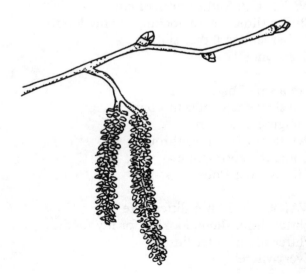

One woolly lamb's tail hanging down
Jiggling, joggling
Blowing in the breeze.

Two woolly lambs' tails hanging down
Jiggling, joggling
Jiggling, joggling
Blowing in the breeze.

Three woolly lambs' tails hanging down
Jiggling, joggling
Jiggling, joggling
Jiggling, joggling
Blowing in the breeze.

Four woolly lambs' tails hanging down
Jiggling, joggling
Jiggling, joggling
Jiggling, joggling
Jiggling, joggling
Blowing in the breeze.

JULIE TONKIN

Lady Spring

TRADITIONAL CIRCLE GAME

Look who's here, it's Lady Spring, Lady Spring, Lady Spring,

Look who's here, it's Lady Spring, Lady Spring is here.

Chorus:
Look who's here, it's Lady Spring,   (*children stand in circle, Lady Spring in the centre*)
Lady Spring, Lady Spring,
Look who's here, it's Lady Spring,
Lady Spring is here.

Who'll come into our wee ring... etc.   (*Lady Spring chooses a partner*)
And dance with Lady Spring?

William will come into our wee ring...etc.
And dance with Lady Spring.   (*keep singing this verse, both choosing a partner,
                                        till all children are dancing*)

Come with me said Lady Spring...etc.   (*everyone sing and dance*)
We're off to dance and sing.

Lily Lily Wallflowers

TRADITIONAL CIRCLE GAME

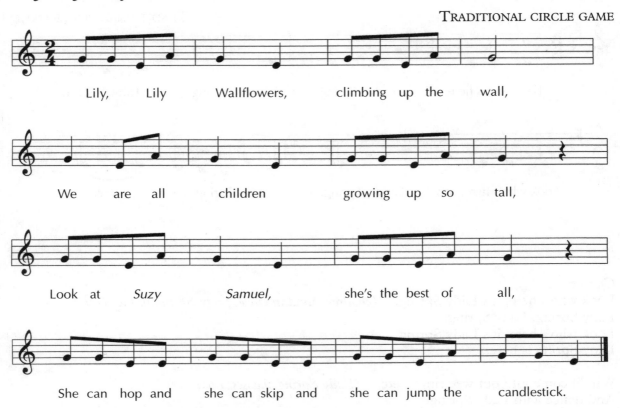

Lily, Lily Wallflowers, climbing up the wall,

We are all children growing up so tall,

Look at *Suzy Samuel,* she's the best of all,

She can hop and she can skip and she can jump the candlestick.

Lily, Lily Wallflowers, climbing up the wall,
We are all children growing up so tall,
Look at *Suzy Samuel,* she's the best of all,
She can hop and she can skip and she can jump the candlestick.

*Children stand in a circle singing. One child is in
the centre, and dances when her name is sung.*

A nettle

Hitty Pitty within the wall,
Hitty Pitty without the wall;
If you touch Hitty Pitty,
Hitty Pitty will bite you.

TRADITIONAL

Shrove Tuesday and Ash Wednesday

Shrove Tuesday, Ash Wednesday

CD TRACK 9

TRADITIONAL

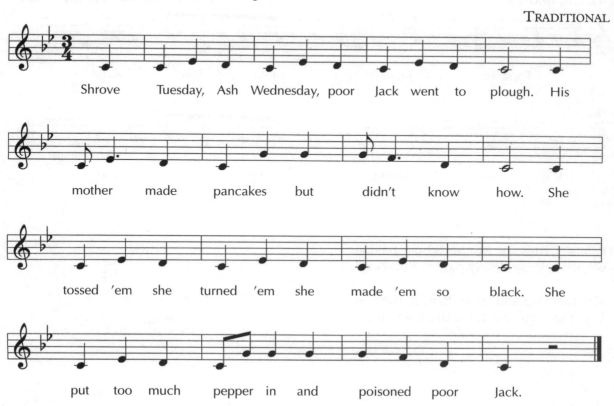

Shrove Tuesday, Ash Wednesday, poor Jack went to plough.
His mother made pancakes but didn't know how.
She tossed 'em she turned 'em she made 'em so black.
She put too much pepper in and poisoned poor Jack.

I use this song to make a little game for children, using a china mixing bowl, a wooden spoon, and some sweets, e.g. Minstrels. Sit the children on the floor round the bowl. Put sweets in the bowl and explain that these are the burnt, peppered pancakes. As everyone sings the song, each child takes their turn to tap round the edge of the bowl with the spoon, in time with the music. At the end of the song, whoever is sitting where the spoon has just tapped, it is their turn to get a 'pancake'. They then become the tapper, until everyone has had a turn. Thus you get to sing the song many times without anyone getting bored, you are practising keeping the beat, and having fun.

Pancake Tuesday

CD TRACK 10

WORDS: ANON.

MUSIC: CANDY VERNEY

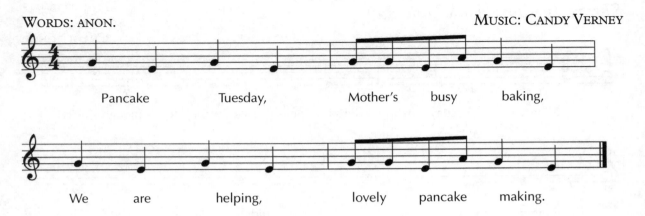

Pancake Tuesday, Mother's busy baking,
We are helping, lovely pancake making.

Mix them up and drop them in the pan,
Toss them up and catch them if you can.

Easter

Hot Cross Buns

CD TRACK 11

TRADITIONAL

Hot cross buns,   hot cross buns,   one a penny, two a penny, hot cross buns.

If you have no daughters give them to your sons. One a penny two a penny, hot cross buns.

Hot cross buns, hot cross buns,
One a penny, two a penny,
Hot cross buns.
If you have no daughters
Give them to your sons.
One a penny, two a penny
Hot cross buns.

*On Good Friday we'd go up the road and buy
some hot cross buns. And all the way up the
road we'd be singing, stepping into the squares
of the pavements.*

Five little eggs in a nest of straw
One egg hatched and then there were four.
Four little eggs in a nest in a tree
One egg hatched and then there were three.
Three little eggs all speckled blue
One egg hatched and then there were two
Two little eggs from where little chicks come
One egg hatched and then there was one.
One little egg lying in the sun
One egg hatched and then there were none.

TRADITIONAL

13

Birds and animals

The winter now is over

CD TRACK 12

TRANS. KATHERINE F. ROHRBOUGH

TRADITIONAL SWISS

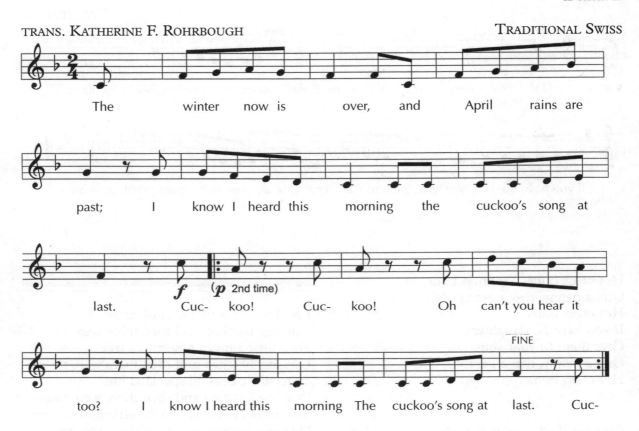

The winter now is over, and April rains are past; I know I heard this morning the cuckoo's song at last. Cuc- koo! Cuc- koo! Oh can't you hear it too? I know I heard this morning The cuckoo's song at last. Cuc-

The winter now is over,
And April rains are past;
I know I heard this morning
The cuckoo's song at last.
Cuckoo! Cuckoo!
Oh can't you hear it too?
I know I heard this morning
The cuckoo's song at last.
Cuckoo! Cuckoo!
Oh can't you hear it too?
I know I heard this morning
The cuckoo's song at last.

Cuckoo, cuckoo, messenger clear

CD TRACK 13

TRADITIONAL GERMAN

Cuckoo, cuckoo, messenger clear, what are you singing,

What are you bringing? Spring-time, spring-time, spring-time is near.

Cuckoo, cuckoo, messenger clear,
What are you singing,
What are you bringing?
Spring-time, spring-time,
Spring-time is near.

Cuckoo, cuckoo, sounding so clear,
Winter is over,
Pink grows the clover,
Spring-time, spring-time,
Spring-time is near.

Cuckoo, cuckoo, sing through the land.
Gladly we hear you
Now we are near you.
Listen, listen,
Spring is at hand.

The cuckoo comes in April
And sings her song in May
In the middle of June, another tune
And then she flies away.

TRADITIONAL

You can make this into a game that children love: two grown ups swing a willing child, one holding her hands, one her feet. Swing her rhythmically to the rhyme, then on the word 'away', throw her gently on to a sofa. For older children, it makes a good throwing game, using a ball or bean bag.

The Bird's Nest

CD TRACK 14

ADAPTED BY CANDY VERNEY*

A little bird built a warm nest in a tree, and laid some blue eggs in it – one, two and three. And

then very glad and delighted was she, very glad and delighted was she.

A little bird built a warm nest in a tree,
And laid some blue eggs in it – one, two and three.
And then very glad and delighted was she,
Very glad and delighted was she.

She spread her soft wings on them all the day long,
To warm them, and guard them, her love was so strong;
And her mate fed her worms, and sang her a song,
Fed her worms, and sang her a song.

And after a while, but how long I can't tell,
The little ones broke one by one from their shell,
And their mother was pleased, and she loved them well,
She was pleased, and she loved them well.

* Adapted by Candy Verney from traditional
  English tune, *The frost is all over.*

Little bird

CD TRACK 15

WORDS: NICOLA WICKSTEED   MUSIC: CANDY VERNEY

p sing very busily

Little bird make your nest. There's no time for a rest.

mp

Lay your eggs, five or six, keep them warm. Hatch your chicks.

mf

Little chicks eat and grow, learn to fly. And off you go!

Little bird
Make your nest.
There's no time
For a rest.
Lay your eggs,
Five or six,
Keep them warm.
Hatch your chicks.
Little chicks
Eat and grow
Learn to fly.
And off you go!

Ladybird, ladybird,
Fly away home,
Your house is on fire,
Your children are gone.
All except one,
And her name is Ann
And she has crept under
The frying pan.
TRADITIONAL

*Children love snuggling under a muslin or silk
cloth, so I have included several games where
this can happen! With this well-known nursery
rhyme, the child/children run about; then they
crouch down together, and the adult floats a
cloth (frying pan) over them.*

Little red robin

CD TRACK 16

WORDS AND MUSIC: CANDY VERNEY

Little red robin up in the tree, little red robin fly down to me.

Little red robin up in the tree,
Little red robin fly down to me.

Hear the blackbird sing

CD TRACK 17

TRADITIONAL

Hear the blackbird sing each little song he sings and

then hark how he sings it over a - gain.

Hear the blackbird sing
Each little song he sings and then
Hark how he sings it over again.

Two little blackbirds singing in the sun,
One flew away and then there was one;
One little blackbird, very black and tall,
He flew away and then there was the wall.
One little brick wall lonely in the rain,
Waiting for the blackbirds to come and sing again.

ANON.

Chook chook

WORDS: TRADITIONAL

MUSIC: CANDY VERNEY

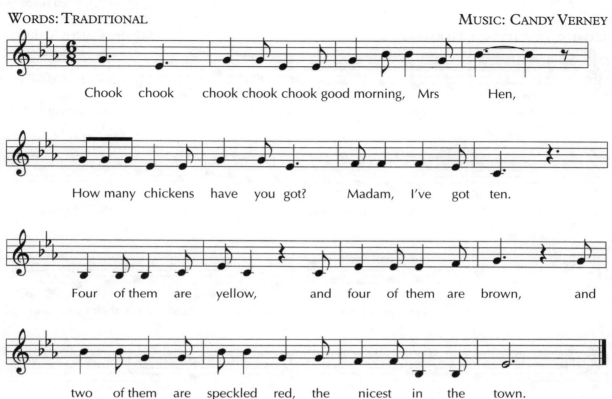

Chook   chook   chook chook chook good morning,   Mrs   Hen,

How many chickens   have   you got?   Madam,   I've   got   ten.

Four   of them   are   yellow,   and   four   of them   are   brown,   and

two   of them   are   speckled   red,   the   nicest   in   the   town.

Chook chook chook chook chook
Good morning, Mrs Hen,
How many chickens have you got?
Madam, I've got ten.
Four of them are yellow,
And four of them are brown,
And two of them are speckled red,
The nicest in the town.

Hickety, pickety, my black hen,
She lays eggs for gentlemen;
Gentlemen come everyday
To see what my black hen doth lay.

TRADITIONAL

Magpie, magpie, flutter and flee,
Turn up your tail and good luck come to me.
One for sorrow, two for joy,
Three for a girl, four for a boy,
Five for silver, six for gold,
Seven for a secret never to be told.

TRADITIONAL

My pigeon house

CD TRACK 19

WORDS: TRADITIONAL GERMAN

MUSIC: CANDY VERNEY

in a free rhythm

My pigeon house I open wide
And set my pigeons free.
They fly around on every side
Up to the highest tree.
Then they come back at evening
And close their eyes and sing:
Croo, croo, croo, croo,
Croo, croo, croo, croo,
Croo, croo, croo, croo, croo, croo.

Adult sits on low stool, wrapped in light blue or white cloth or sheet. Children at her feet. Adult opens her arms and the 'pigeons' fly around. The adult 'flies' too, then comes back to her seat. When the pigeons have returned, she gently floats the cloth over the 'nesting pigeons'.

Dilly dilly duck

TRADITIONAL FRENCH

Dilly dilly duck, dilly hey hey ho! All the little ducks waddle in a row.

Some are white and some are yellow, everyone a pretty fellow, waddle to the water and in you go.

Dilly dilly duck,
Dilly hey hey ho!
All the little ducks waddle in a row.
Some are white and some are yellow,
Everyone a pretty fellow,
Waddle to the water and in you go.

Gray goose and gander,
Waft your wings together,
And carry the good king's daughter
Over the one-strand river.

TRADITIONAL

Coo-coo-pigeons
Would you like some peas?
Here you are and there you are
As many as you please.

Coo-coo-pigeons
Was your dinner good?
Here you go and there you go
And off into the wood.

FROM JAPAN

Woodpecker

Drum a drum drum
Spring is here
Spring is here
Woodpecker tapping at the old brown tree
Drum a drum drum
Drum a drum drum.

JULIE TONKIN

Caterpillar

WORDS AND MUSIC: JULIE TONKIN

Creeping creeping long the twig I raise my head, my back, my toes

Slowly slowly hair by hair My cat-er-pil-lar body goes.

Creeping creeping long the twig
I raise my head, my back, my toes
Slowly slowly hair by hair
My caterpillar body goes.

Caterpillar

Caterpillar on a twig,
Eat your leaves so you'll grow big.
When you're big, away you'll creep,
Make your bed and go to sleep.
You will change as time goes by
And wake up as a butterfly.

NICOLA WICKSTEED

The Tickle Rhyme

"Who's that tickling my back?" said the wall.
"Me," said a small
Caterpillar, "I'm learning
To crawl."
(tickle the child's back)

ANNE SERRAILLIER

Little Hare

CD TRACK 22

WORDS: TRADITIONAL GERMAN

MUSIC: CANDY VERNEY

See the little hare is fast asleep, fast asleep.

Little hare O are you ill, that you lie so quiet and still?

Hop little hare, hop little hare, hop, hop, hop, hop, hop everywhere.

See the little hare is fast asleep, fast asleep.   *crouch on floor*
Little hare O are you ill,
That you lie so quiet and still?
Hop little hare, hop little hare,   *jump up and hop*
Hop, hop, hop, hop, hop everywhere.

The Digger

I'm a digger
And I'm alive.
I'm not the kind of digger
You can get in and drive.
To move my shovels,
I don't need a control.
I'm a tunnel digging,
Worm catching,
Velvety mole.
                NICOLA WICKSTEED

Dot to frog

CD TRACK 23

WORDS: NICOLA WICKSTEED   MUSIC: CANDY VERNEY

Wriggledy wriggledy   wriggle a lot: Stuck in the jelly,   little black dot.

Waggledy waggledy   waggle and roll: Swim in the water,   little tadpole.

Jumpitty jumpitty jumpitty jog: Jump in the meadow, little green frog.

Wriggledy wriggledy
Wriggle a lot:
Stuck in the jelly,
Little black dot.

Waggledy waggledy
Waggle and roll:
Swim in the water,
Little tadpole.

Jumpitty jumpitty
Jumpitty jog:
Jump in the meadow,
Little green frog.

Frog

A frog is leaping: hoppity hop,
Reaches the pond: stoppity stop,
Dives straight in: ploppity plop,
Lays jellied eggs: sloppity slop!
              NICOLA WICKSTEED

Herdsmaid's song

TRADITIONAL NORWEGIAN

Nanny goat, Billy goat, little kid with fluffy coat,

Rosie, Dolly, Peggy, Molly, Old Long Legs,

faster

Frisky, Bonny May, and the Player on the mountain.

Nanny goat, Billy goat,
Little kid with fluffy coat,
Rosie, Dolly,
Peggy, Molly,
Old Long Legs, Frisky,
Bonny May,
And the Player on the mountain.

*The strong rhythm of this song lends itself to
dandling, clapping and marching.*

Spring Lambs

It is a most exciting thing
To see the new born lambs of spring;
Yet they that scamper, chase and leap,
Soon grow and slow down into sheep.

NICOLA WICKSTEED

May woods and weather

Here's a branch of snowy may

CD TRACK 25

TRADITIONAL DUTCH

Here's a branch of   snowy may,   a   branch the   fairies   gave   us.

Who would like   to dance   today,   with the branch the fairies   gave   us?

Dance   away,   dance   away,   holding high   the   branch of   may.

Dance   away,   dance   away,   holding high   the   branch of   may.

Here's a branch of snowy may,
A branch the fairies gave us.
Who would like to dance today,
With the branch the fairies gave us?
Dance away, dance away,
Holding high the branch of may.
Dance away, dance away,
Holding high the branch of may.

Walking in the woods

WORDS AND MUSIC: ANON.

While walking in the woods one day, in the merry merry month of May, I was

taken by surprise, by a pair of lovely eyes, while walking in the woods one day.

While walking in the woods one day,
In the merry merry month of May,
I was taken by surprise, by a pair of lovely eyes,
While walking in the woods one day.

One child sits in the middle of the circle, hidden under a light cloth.
Everyone else holds hands and walks around, until she reveals her lovely eyes.

The Carpet

I'll show you a carpet;
It looks good.
It's not in the house;
It's out in the wood.
Walk with me
To have a surprise:
A carpet of bluebells
Before your eyes.
NICOLA WICKSTEED

Foxgloves

Lovely foxgloves standing tall
By the old grey crumbling wall,
Could your blooms like tiny mittens
Fit the paws of fox cubs or kittens?
NICOLA WICKSTEED

In and out the dusky bluebells

CD TRACK 27

TRADITIONAL

In and out the dusky bluebells In and out the dusky bluebells

In and out the dusky bluebells Won't you be my partner?

Pitter patter pitter patter on your shoulder Pitter patter pitter patter on your shoulder

Pitter patter pitter patter on your shoulder Won't you be my partner?

In and out the dusky bluebells
In and out the dusky bluebells
In and out the dusky bluebells
Won't you be my partner?

Pitter patter pitter patter on your shoulder
Pitter patter pitter patter on your shoulder
Pitter patter pitter patter on your shoulder
Won't you be my partner?

Some children stand in circle, holding hands and making arches. A line of other children hold hands and weave in and out of the circle.

Lightly patter on shoulder.

Rain on the green grass

CD TRACK 28

WORDS: TRADITIONAL   MUSIC: CANDY VERNEY

Rain on the green grass,   *(spread arms low)*
Rain on the tree,   *(lift arms up like tree)*
Rain on the house top,   *(bend arms over head)*
But not on me!   *(cross arms over chest)*

Rain

Pitter-patter, hear it raining?   *(clap hands slowly
                    and lightly, gradually getting faster and louder)*
Slow at first, then faster, faster.
Put on you raincoat,   *(imitate actions)*
Hold up your umbrella,
Pull on your Wellingtons
And splash in the puddles.

LILIAN MCCREA

Rain rain go away, come again another day
Rain rain go away, come again another day
Rain rain go away, little Janey wants to play!

TRADITIONAL

Spring-time goodbye

CD TRACK 29

TRADITIONAL GERMAN

Spring-time good-bye, spring-time good-bye, you may no longer stay,

Summer is on its way, spring-time good-bye, spring-time good-bye.

Spring-time goodbye, spring-time goodbye,
You may no longer stay, summer is on its way
Spring-time goodbye, spring-time goodbye.

Pavements and playgrounds

Hippety hop to the barber's shop

CD TRACK 30

WORDS: TRADITIONAL

MUSIC: CANDY VERNEY

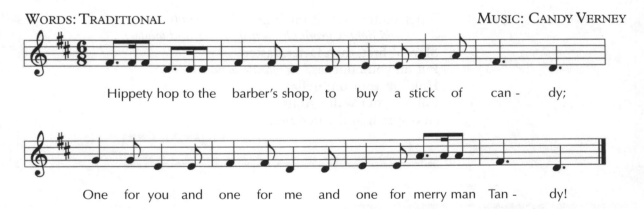

Hippety hop to the barber's shop, to buy a stick of can - dy;

One for you and one for me and one for merry man Tan - dy!

Hippety hop to the barber's shop,
To buy a stick of candy;
One for you and one for me
And one for merry man Tandy!

Make up verses of your own, to match the shops you visit.

30

The Swing

CD TRACK 31

WORDS: ADAPTED FROM A POEM BY MARY I. OSBORN   MUSIC: CANDY VERNEY

Now so high, now so low, up in the air, then down I go.

Up to the sky, down to the ground, I watch the birds fly with - out a sound.

The Swing

Now so high,
Now so low,
Up in the air,
Then down I go.
Up to the sky,
Down to the ground,
I watch the birds fly
Without a sound.

Hippety hippety hop,
Hoppety, hoppety hip,
Let's jump and skip.

I remember singing was really helpful when Annie was a toddler and didn't want to walk any further. I used to sing the above, and we would jump on and off the curb, and she would forget she was tired!

Giving a sense of timing:

I use a well-known, simple nursery rhyme to help Lucy understand time, for instance when I want her to leave the swing as it's time to go. Instead of saying 'Two more minutes' or counting (which she can't relate to), I tell her I will sing Twinkle Twinkle Little Star, *and when I've finished singing it, it will be time to go. This gives her an amount of time she can judge, plus a warning/adjustment time for leaving. Also useful on a long car journey, when we're nearly home, and useful for taking turns.*

See-saw, Margery Daw

CD TRACK 32

TRADITIONAL

See - saw,   Margery Daw,   Jacky shall have a new mas - ter;

He   shall have but a   penny a   day,   Because he can't work any   fas -   ter.

See-saw, Margery Daw,
Jacky shall have a new master;
He shall have but a penny a day,
Because he can't work any faster.

The king of France, the king of France,
With forty thousand men,
Oh, they all went up the hill, and so –
They all came down again.

TRADITIONAL

I was working in a playgroup, and one particular boy was always very withdrawn and isolated, sad. There was a possibility of his going into care, because of family disputes. One day I noticed a twinkle in his eye while we sang Grand old Duke of York. His sense of rhythm was better than anybody else's. Incredibly, he responded when I invited him to 'lead the other soldiers'. He smiled, stood straight and walked beautifully. After that, music time was a special time for him, an oasis for emotional relaxation from outside challenges. His self assurance grew, and from then on, other children wanted to play with him.

See-saw sacradown

CD TRACK 33

WORDS: TRADITIONAL

MUSIC: CANDY VERNEY

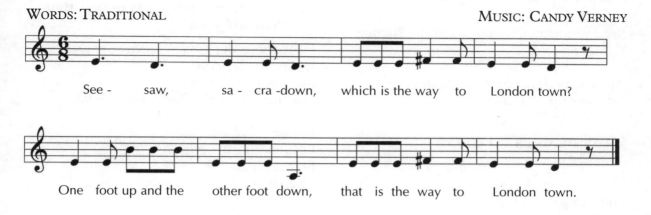

See - saw, sa - cra -down, which is the way to London town?

One foot up and the other foot down, that is the way to London town.

See-saw, sacradown,
Which is the way to London town?
One foot up and the other foot down,
That is the way to London town.

My Wellington boots go
Thump-thump, thump-thump, *(beat loudly on the floor with feet)*
My leather shoes go
Pit-pat, pit-pat, *(beat softly)*
My brand new trainers go
Squeak-squeak, squeak-squeak, *(make a squeaky noise)*
But my bare feet
Make no noise at all. *(beat with feet, making no noise at all)*

ADAPTED FROM A POEM BY LILIAN McCREA

Spring activities

See Introduction 'Singing and the Natural World' on page x.

All plants listed have a particular interest for children.

EASY PLANTS TO GROW

Bulbs

Snowdrops – *bulbs poisonous*
Crocuses
Hyacinths
Daffodils – *bulbs and leaves are poisonous, also an irritant*
Narcissus   "   "
Bluebells – *poisonous and irritant*
Tulips – *irritant*

Bulbs can be planted in a pot in autumn. Keep in a cool place to grow slowly, and bring into the living area just before flowering. Alternatively, plant in the garden in autumn and watch them flower in spring.

Perennials
– these will flower year after year

Primrose – *poisonous and irritant*
Primula   "   "
Polyanthus
Lungwort – *Pulmonaria. The first pink and blue flower of the year. Irritant*
Osteospermum
Columbine – *Aquilegia. Also self-seeds*
Comfrey – *interesting rough, furry leaves, and a beautiful flower which changes colour as it unfolds. Irritant*

Annual and biennial seeds to sow, that will then self-seed

Foxglove – *all parts are poisonous if eaten*
Honesty – *Lunaria*
Marigold – *Calendula*
Nasturtium – *will self-seed only in milder climates*
Borage – *irritant*
Love-in-a-mist – *Nigella*
Eschscholtzia
Valerian – *Centranthus ruber*
Forget-me-not
Pansy – *the flower looks like a face*

Flowering shrubs and trees

Forsythia – *earliest yellow flowers in spring*
Philadelphus – *wonderful scent*
Honeysuckle – *there is a little tongue inside that is sweet, and children love to suck it*
Pussy willow – *Salix caprea. The furry buds are a favourite*
Hazel – *produces catkins in February*

Herbs for their scent, and also to eat

Rosemary
Lavender
Chives
Marjoram, especially the golden variety: origanum vulgare 'Aurea'
Mint: *there are many varieties, each with a different fragrance. Here are some:*
  Spearmint
  Apple mint
  Ginger mint
  Lemon mint
  Corsican mint
  Pineapple mint

Pennyroyal – *will grow flat in the corner of a path. When rubbed, it gives off a strong aromatic scent. Poisonous*

Lemon balm

Thyme

Angelica – *the stalks are crystallised and used as cake decoration*

Feverfew – *more medicinal than culinary*

Catmint – *'Six Hills Giant' is wonderfully prolific*

Artemisia – *feathery silver leaves. Medicinal*

Chives – *just pick a stem and chew*

Welsh onion

Things to do in spring

Seed sprouting

All sorts of seeds can be grown on a saucer, or in a jam jar:

    Mustard and cress

    Bean sprouts – many varieties

    Broad beans

See *Mustard and Cress* ('In the garden', Summer, page 51).

Easter garden

Take an old plate, and cover it with a layer of soil. Make a beautiful garden with moss, flowers, twigs for trees, little stones and what ever else you find. And don't forget the Easter eggs!

Vegetables to grow

With a little patch of land or even a window box, you can grow radishes, and tasty spring lettuces!

See *Savez-vous planter les choux?* ('In the garden', Summer, page 52).

Blindfold tree hugging

In a park with several trees close together, or in a wood:
Blindfold the child, and take him to a tree. Encourage him to smell, feel and touch it, to rub his cheek against the bark, listen to the sound of the leaves. Then guide him away from the tree, take off the blindfold, and the child tries to find the tree that he was feeling.

SPRING

Stinging nettle soup

A delicious soup can be made with the first green shoots of spring, very nutritious too. Children will be curious that the sting is annulled by cooking.

Plant a sunflower

Plant in a pot, then transplant into the ground when around 30cm high.

I can remember my father's excitement when he discovered he could grow sunflowers. He grew them up the wall of our house. They reached the first floor window. We dried one by hanging it in the garage: it was there all my childhood!

Sunflower grow, sunflower grow
Right up the wall and reaching the window
Sunflower grow, sunflower grow....

Make up your own verses.

PLANTS TO LOOK OUT FOR
– around parks and in the countryside

Trees

The sticky buds of chestnut trees
Hazel catkins
Pussy willow
Hawthorn – *the very young leaves are edible, and used to be called 'bread and cheese'*

See 'Useful trees' in Autumn section, page 84.

Smaller plants

It is important to properly identify edible plants. Some wild plants are poisonous. Be sure you know the plant well before you eat it.

Garlic mustard – *grows along the sides of country roads, and in waste places. Edible, and tastes of both garlic and mustard*
Wild garlic – *common in woods and on banks. Edible. The leaves have a mild garlic flavour*
Wood sorrel – *edible. The leaves taste lemony and delicious*
Bluebells – *inedible*
Cow parsley – *inedible*

Do not pick any but the commonest wild flowers. It is illegal, as their numbers have greatly diminished.

Count the wild flowers

Some older children will love to count the number of species of flower in a hedge. There will hopefully be at least six in any hedge. Or use a counting song to count the numbers of a particular flower – see the companion volume to this one: *The Singing Day* – reference in the Bibliography.

36

Summer

Sing a song of summer days,
Leafy nooks and shady ways.

J. W. FOLEY

Animals

Busy bee

WORDS AND MUSIC: CANDY VERNEY

I'm busy, busy, busy said the bee, I shan't be home for dinner or tea, It takes me hours and hours to visit all the flowers, I'm

I'm busy, busy, busy said the bee,
I shan't be home for dinner or tea,
It takes me hours and hours
To visit all the flowers,
I'm busy, busy, busy said the bee.

Game: Children stand in a circle with hands cupped as flowers. One child, the bee, 'busies' around them, 'sucking nectar from each flower'.

Traditional counting rhyme

Bumblebee, bumblebee,
Stung a man upon his knee,
Stung a pig upon his snout,
Goodness me, if you're not out.

A finger game

Here is the beehive   (cup one hand inside the other)
But where are the bees?
Hidden away where nobody sees.
Soon they are creeping out of the hive,
One, two, three, four, five   (let fingers out one by one)
Buzz, buzz, buzz!

TRADITIONAL

Butterfly

CD TRACK 35

MUSIC: ARRANGED BY CANDY VERNEY ★

See the little butter - fly as she gai - ly flutters by,

lands up - on a butter - cup, and then once more goes flying up.

See the little butterfly
As she gaily flutters by,
Lands upon a buttercup,
And then once more goes flying up.

Welcome little butterfly
We will love you as you fly.
Safely, safely you will come
With your message from the sun.

*One child dances around the circle, flapping her
butterfly wings (a soft yellow cloth).
On 'lands upon a buttercup', she lets the cloth
rest gently on someone's head.*

*At nursery, when the children had a
rest, I'd cover them with a silk scarf.
When it came to waking up, they'd all
get up with their scarves and wave
them about like butterflies*

Oh No!

Oh no!
Off you go!
You ripped my bin bag,
Big bad crow.
You ripped my bin bag,
What a disgrace!
Just look at this rubbish
All over the place!

NICOLA WICKSTEED

★ Arranged by Candy Verney from English
dance tune – *Winster Gallop.*

Snail

TRADITIONAL

Four and twenty tailors went to catch a snail, the best man amongst them durst not touch her tail; she

put out her horns like a little Kyloe cow. Run, tailors, run, or she'll catch you all e'en now.

Four and twenty tailors
Went to catch a snail,
The best man amongst them
Durst not touch her tail;
She put out her horns
Like a little Kyloe cow.
Run, tailors, run,
Or she'll catch you all e'en now.

Waggle fingers on one hand for the tailors and make a fist with the other hand for the snail.

Barn Owl

Barn owl of the night,
Hover in your silent flight.
Pounce and catch a mouse or two,
Your hungry chicks depend on you.
                    NICOLA WICKSTEED

Thank you, pretty cow, that made
Tasty milk to soak my bread,
Every day and every night
Warm and fresh and sweet and white.

Where the purple violet grows,
Where the bubbling water flows,
Where the grass is fresh and fine,
Pretty cow, go there and dine.
                    JANE TAYLOR

Swifts and swallows and martins

WORDS: NICOLA WICKSTEED

MUSIC: CANDY VERNEY

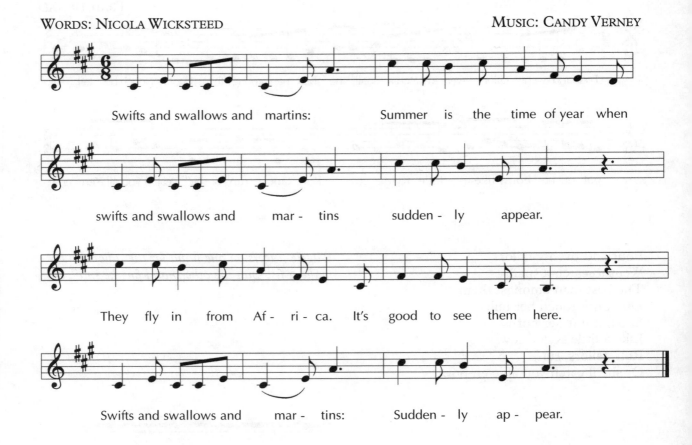

Swifts and swallows and martins: Summer is the time of year when

swifts and swallows and mar - tins sudden - ly appear.

They fly in from Af - ri - ca. It's good to see them here.

Swifts and swallows and mar - tins: Sudden - ly ap - pear.

Swifts and swallows and martins:
Summer is the time of year
When swifts and swallows and martins
Suddenly appear.
They fly in from Africa.
It's good to see them here.
Swifts and swallows and martins:
Suddenly appear.

Chicka Chicka

CD TRACK 38

WORDS: NICOLA WICKSTEED   MUSIC: CANDY VERNEY

Chicka chicka, chicka chicka; what makes the sound
Rubbing its legs in the grass on the ground?
Chicka chicka grasshopper, jump from my hand.
Go and join a chicka chicka grasshopper band.
Chicka chicka chicka chicka grasshopper band!

Over in the meadow

TRADITIONAL

Over in the meadow, in the sand, in the sun, lived a

dear mother Toad and her little toady one. Hop! said the mother, hop!

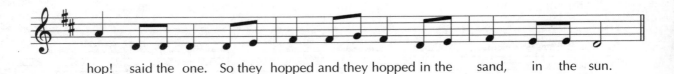

hop! said the one. So they hopped and they hopped in the sand, in the sun.

Over in the meadow, in the sand, in the sun,
Lived a dear mother Toad and her little toady one.
Hop! said the mother, hop! hop! said the one.
So they hopped and they hopped in the sand, in the sun.

Over in the meadow, where the stream runs blue,
Lived a dear mother Fish and her little fishes two.
Swim! said the mother, swim! swim! said the two.
So they swam and they leapt where the stream runs blue.

Over in the meadow, in the big oak tree,
Lived a dear mother Blackbird and her little birdies three.
Sing! said the mother, sing! sing! said the three
So they sang and were glad in the hole in the tree.

Over in the meadow, in the sand on the shore,
Lived a mother Water Rat and her little ratties four.
Dive!, said the mother, dive! dive! said the four.
So they dived and they burrowed in the reeds on the shore.

Over in the meadow, in a snug beehive,
Lived a mother Honeybee and her little honeys five.
Buzz! said the mother, buzz! buzz! said the five.
So they buzzed and they hummed in the snug beehive.

Plants and flowers

Buttercups

CD TRACK 40

WORDS: ANON.   MUSIC: CANDY VERNEY

Buttercups golden and gay, sway in the wind all day. They

tickle the nose of the cow as she goes, and they call to the bees, Come a - way.

Buttercups golden and gay,
Sway in the wind all day.
They tickle the nose of the cow as she goes,
And they call to the bees, Come away.

All around the buttercup

CD TRACK 41

TRADITIONAL CIRCLE GAME

All around the buttercup, One two three,   If you want a cheeky lad Just choose me.

All around the buttercup,
One two three,
If you want a cheeky lad
Just choose me.

Children sit in a circle, one child is the buttercup and weaves in and out around the circle. On the last word of the song, he taps the child near to him, who then joins him to make a snake. They hold hands and weave together, until only one child is left, who becomes the buttercup in the centre of the circle and the game begins again.

Lavender's blue

TRADITIONAL

Lav - en - der's blue, dilly dilly, lav - en - der's green,

When I am king, dilly dilly, you shall be queen.

Lavender's blue, dilly dilly,
Lavender's green,
When I am king, dilly dilly,
You shall be queen.

Call up the plough, dilly dilly,
Set them to work,
Some to the plough, dilly dilly,
Some to the cart.

Some to make hay, dilly dilly,
Some to thresh corn,
Whilst you and I, dilly dilly,
Keep ourselves warm.

The dandelion puff
Is a very strange clock,
It doesn't say tick,
And it doesn't say tock.
It hasn't a cuckoo,
It hasn't a chime,
And I really don't think
It can tell me the time!
                MARY K. ROBINSON

Round about the rosebush,
Three steps,
Four steps,
All the little girls and boys
Are sitting
On the doorsteps.
                TRADITIONAL

Harvest

The silver rain, the shining sun,
The fields where scarlet poppies run,
And all the ripples of the wheat
Are in the bread that I do eat.

So when I sit for every meal
And say a grace, I always feel
That I am eating rain and sun,
And fields where scarlet poppies run.
                ALICE C. HENDERSON

This makes a beautiful grace before a meal.

Here we come a-haying

WORDS: EUNICE CLOSE   MUSIC: TRADITIONAL

Here we come a- hay - ing a- hay - ing a- hay - ing,

Here we come a- hay - ing a - mong the leaves so green.

Here we come a-haying
A-haying a-haying,
Here we come a-haying
Among the leaves so green.

Up and down the mower goes,
All the long field over,
Cutting down the long green grass
And the purple clover.

Toss the hay and turn it,
Laid in rows do neatly,
Summer sun a-shining down,
Makes it smell so sweetly.

Rake it into tidy piles
Now the farmer's ready,
Load it on the old hay cart,
Drawn by faithful Neddy.

Down the lane the last load goes,
Hear the swallow calling.
Now at last our work is done,
Night is softly falling.

The actions of the song can be imitated.

Here's a tree in summer
(a grass seed head)

Here's a tree in winter
(pull off the seeds)

Here's a bunch of flowers
*(seeds contained
between fingers)*

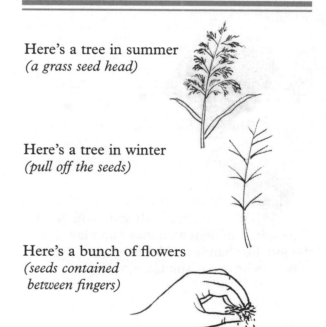

And here's the April showers.
(throw seeds in the air!)

Midsummer's Day

Midsummer's Day, celebrated since ancient times, is the time when the sun reaches its highest point in the sky, and we enjoy our longest day. Many countries, especially in northern latitudes, still celebrate, either on the summer solstice on June 21, or the official Midsummer's Day on June 24, (also called St John's Day). Large communal bonfires are lit,

and festivities go on through the night. Celebrating midsummer provides a counterbalance to the Christmas festivities, held at the opposite time of the year, and therefore unconsciously gives children a feeling of the long rhythms of the year. They love to dress up in golden colours and wear crowns, and make suns on sticks, with streamers.

Tomorrow is Midsummer's Day

CD TRACK 44

WORDS AND MUSIC: CANDY VERNEY

To - morrow is Mid - summer's Day, the spirits of light all dance and play. So

join our hands and let us sing, the sun he is our shining king.

Tomorrow is Midsummer's Day
    [Or: Today it is… It soon will be…]
The spirits of light all dance and play.
So join our hands and let us sing,
The sun he is our shining king.

Make a little throne – just a chair with a yellow cloth over will do – and a gold crown.

Children can take turns to be the Sun King, and sit on the throne, while others dance around him.

Midsummer's Day is a royal day

CD TRACK 45

WORDS: NICOLA WICKSTEED   MUSIC: ARRANGED BY CANDY VERNEY *

Midsummer's Day is a ro - yal day. King Sun will pro - gress on his ro - yal way to the

ve - ry top of the sky where he will shine down his blessings on you and me.

La la la ... etc.

Midsummer's Day is a royal day.
King Sun will progress on his royal way
To the very top of the sky where he
Will shine down his blessings on you and me.
La la la ... etc.

* Arranged by Candy Verney from tune
Cornish Floral Dance

Shadows go round

CD TRACK 46

WORDS AND MUSIC: ANON.

Shadows go round,　　shadows go round,　　shadows go round with　　me.

Skip and dance in the　　sun - shine,　　all the way round with　　me.

Shadows go round, shadows go round,
Shadows go round with me.
Skip and dance in the sunshine,
All the way round with me.

Long Days

I like to play in the garden
I like to play in the park.
I play out longer in the summer because
It takes longer for it to get dark.

NICOLA WICKSTEED

In the garden

CD TRACK 47

Cotton field

TRADITIONAL JAMAICAN

I pick up me hoe an' I go, I pick up me hoe an' I go – o – o, come wid me an' help hoe a row, an' we'll hoe an' we'll hoe an' we'll hoe.

I pick up me hoe an' I go,
I pick up me hoe an' I go – o – o,
Come wid me an' help hoe a row,
An' we'll hoe an' we'll hoe an' we'll hoe.

I hoe where de young cabbage grow,
I hoe where de young cabbage grow – ow – ow,
O help hoe a young cabbage row,
An' we'll hoe an' we'll hoe an' we'll hoe.

Mustard and cress, mustard and cress
Which tastes the hottest and which do you like best?
TRADITIONAL

Savez-vous planter les choux?

CD TRACK 48

TRADITIONAL FRENCH

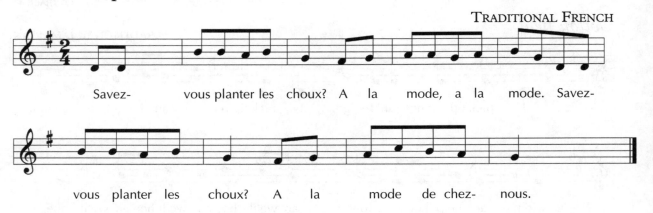

Savez- vous planter les choux? A la mode, a la mode. Savez-

vous planter les choux? A la mode de chez- nous.

Savez-vous planter les choux?
A la mode, a la mode.
Savez-vous planter les choux?
A la mode de chez-nous.

On les plante avec le doigt
A la mode, a la mode.
On les plante avec le doigt
A la mode de chez-nous.

English version
Can you plant some radishes?
In the garden, in the garden.
Can you plant some radishes?
Crunchy, hot and red to eat.

Can you plant some lettuces?
In the garden, in the garden,
Can you plant some lettuces?
Then we'll eat them fresh and sweet.

Old Mister Rabbit

WORDS AND MUSIC: K. FORRAI

Old Mister Rab - bit, you've got a mighty ha - bit of

jumping in my gar - den and eating all my cabbage!

Old Mister Rabbit, you've got a mighty habit
Of jumping in my garden and eating all my
cabbage!

Two children form a gate with upraised arms.
The other children walk in a line through the
gate. On the word 'cabbage', the gate comes
down trapping 'Mister Rabbit', who then joins
one or other side of the gate.

Robert Rabbit

Robert Rabbit, please do not
Hop into my veggie plot.
Think of all the veg I've got.
If you could, you'd eat the lot.
One lettuce
Two three four;
Five and six
And then some more:
Seven lettuces
Eight nine ten;
Home for a rest
Then you're back again!

Stop it! Stop it!
Hop it! Hop it!

Robert Rabbit, please do not etc...
(radish, cabbage, carrots etc)

NICOLA WICKSTEED

53

Raspberries hide

CD TRACK 50

WORDS: NICOLA WICKSTEED   MUSIC: CANDY VERNEY

Rasp - ber - ries hide un - der - neath the leaves.

That's why I de - cide to ask the chil - dren, "Please

Help me to pick them; the rea - son why is this:

Chil - dren find the ber - ries that the grown- ups miss."

Raspberries hide
Underneath the leaves.
That's why I decide
To ask the children, "Please
Help me to pick them;
The reason why is this:
Children find the berries
That the grownups miss."

Seaside and holidays

Pebbles

CD TRACK 51

WORDS: EDITH KING   MUSIC: CANDY VERNEY

Pebbles, pebbles, pebbles, for miles and miles and miles: A sloping bank of pebbles round all the British Isles.

Pebbles, pebbles, pebbles,
For miles and miles and miles:
A sloping bank of pebbles
Round all the British Isles.

Hearken in my tiny ear

CD TRACK 52

WORDS: JULIE TONKIN   MUSIC: CANDY VERNEY

Hearken in my tiny ear, hold the shell so close, so near, Stories of the sea I hear, from the shell up - on my ear.

Hearken in my tiny ear,
Hold the shell so close, so near,
Stories of the sea I hear,
From the shell upon my ear.

The Kayak Song

CD TRACK 53

WORDS: LUCY DIAMOND

MUSIC: CANDY VERNEY

pp
Over the dark water   see the kayak steal;   Father's going searching for the fish and seal.

mp
Will he have good hunting out beyond the floe? He may see a bear there, 'mid the ice and snow.

pp
Over the dark water,   see the kayak steal.   Softly – lest you frighten hidden fish and seal.

Over the dark water
See the kayak steal;
Father's going searching
For the fish and seal.

Will he have good hunting
Out beyond the floe?
He may see a bear there
'Mid the ice and snow.

Over the dark water
See the kayak steal.
Softly – lest you frighten
Hidden fish and seal.

Jumping waves

One two three and four,
Hold my hand mum,
Five six seven wait,
Here it comes, the GIANT one.
JULIE TONKIN

We were always told, as children, that the seventh wave is always the biggest one. To this day I still think that and have counted the waves with my own children to the same effect.

Climbing a rock

CD TRACK 54

WORDS: JULIE TONKIN   MUSIC: CANDY VERNEY

Sun warmed shiny rock,   up the side I clamber,   hold the sticking-out bit tight,

slower and slower   *normal speed*

If   I pull I might, I might reach the, reach the…very top. Sun warmed shiny rock, down the side I clamber,

slower and slower

Put my foot in   little cracks,   if I slide I might, I might   touch the, touch the… sandy ground.

Sun warmed shiny rock,
Up the side I clamber,
Hold the sticking-out bit tight,
If I pull I might, I might
Reach the, reach the….
Very top.

Sun warmed shiny rock,
Down the side I clamber,
Put my foot in little cracks,
If I slide I might, I might
Touch the, touch the…
Sandy ground.

Form a ring with a group of children. 'Clamber up' the rock, gradually going into the middle of the circle.

When you reach the top, all arms are stretched up in the centre.

Then slowly 'clamber down' again, till you return to the original ring.

Shrimping

CD TRACK 55

WORDS: JULIE TONKIN   MUSIC: ADAPTED BY CANDY VERNEY *

In the middle of my pool I'm sure there lives a crab and

I would like to take my net and with it I will grab... my crab.

In the middle of my pool
I'm sure there lives a crab
And I would like to take my net
And with it I will grab...
My crab.

Underneath that little rock
A shrimp or two they swim
And I would like to take my net
And with it I will win...
My shrimp.

So carefully I stretch my net
Across the rocky pool
And I have bent myself too far
And with a splash I fall...
Right in!

Buckets and spades

Buckets and spades, buckets and spades
And digging and messing with sand;
And tipping and shaping
And patting and making
A castle that's ever so grand.

NICOLA WICKSTEED

*   Adapted by Candy Verney from an
    American folksong.

Summer activities

See Introduction 'Singing and the Natural World', page x.

All plants listed have a particular interest for children.

EASY PLANTS TO GROW

Perennials

Lady's mantle – *Alchemilla mollis*
Thrift – *Armeria*
Fairies thimbles – *Campanula cochleariifolia*
Canterbury bells – *Campanula medium*
Echinacea
Coreopsis
Rudbeckia
Periwinkle – *Vinca. Poisonous*
Bird's-foot-trefoil – *'eggs and bacon' (often found in lawns)*

Yellow flowers for midsummer festivities:

Buttercup
Oxeye daisy
Yellow loosestrife – *Lysimachia punctata*
Hypericum

Grasses

Children will put grasses to many uses. They can be plaited, made into animals, bracelets, bedding, or just appreciated for the variety and shape of their seeds. If you have a lawn, let a part of it grow long and see what is there.

Shrubs and trees

Fuchsia – *the flowers are 'dancing ladies'*
Rose – *a useful climbing variety that is thornless is Zephirine Drouhin*
Buddleia – *attracts butterflies, sometimes called the Butterfly Bush*
Snowberry – *Symphoricarpos rivularis. Put the 'snowballs' on the ground and pop them.*

For scent

Choisya ternata
Daphne – *poisonous*
Honeysuckle – *Lonicera*
Jasmine – *Jasminum officinalis*
Lilac – *Syringa*
Philadelphus
Viburnum
Nicotiana, *for evening fragrance. Poisonous and irritant*
Stock – *Matthiola, for day and evening fragrance*

To attract butterflies

Alyssum saxatile
Thrift – *Armeria*
Michaelmas daisy – *Aster*
Calamintha
Valerian – *Centranthus ruber*
Coreopsis
Echinacea
Buddleia
Escallonia

For their seedheads

Poppy
Honesty
Rose hips
Tall grasses
Teasel

Soft fruits to grow

These bushes will sit in a corner of the garden. They'll need a bit of annual pruning, mulching and fertilising, but not much more, once they are established, and you can have the fun of picking your own fruit.

Blackcurrants
Redcurrants
Raspberries
Strawberries
Gooseberries – *choose a variety that is sweet enough to eat straight from the bush*
Wild strawberries – *these will flourish in any dry or dusty or shady corner, along paths, along steps, or under trees. They will generously spread along the edges, and provide hidden sweet delights to any little person who discovers them. The berries will continue all summer and into the autumn, and need no maintenance, except very occasional weeding.*

To train against a wall

Blackberries
Wineberries – *children love their stickiness!*
Loganberries

Into the jungle: very large plants

Angelica
Cardoon
Elecampane – *Inula helenium*
Gunnera – *needs a boggy area*

Things to do in summer

Dandelion clocks

Count how many puffs it takes to blow all the seeds off the head. See poem on page 46.

Elderflower cordial

A delicious cordial can be made from elderflowers, water, sugar and lemons, that will last all year – if you don't drink it! One recipe can be found in *Family, Festivals and Food* (see bibliography).

Blow the grass

Place fat blade of grass between thumb and forefinger, and blow through.

Grass bracelet

Pick several strands of long but flexible grass. Tie together at one end, with another piece of grass. Divide into three, and start plaiting. When it is long enough, bind in the same way and tie the two ends together.

Honesty butterfly

- *5-6cm stalk of cow parsley, hogweed,* ★ *angelica or sweet corn (any plant that has a hollow fairly strong stem)*
- *four honesty (Lunaria) dried seed heads*
- *for the antennae: a grass stem, or strips off the stalk being used for the body*
- *a pin*

Using the pin, make four holes in the sides of the stem. Insert the stem of the honesty. For the antennae, wind a grass stalk around a pencil to make it curly, and insert it into the top of the stem. You can also use a strip peeled off the cow parsley stem.

Poppy seed head dolls

The seed head of a poppy looks just like a doll's head, with a hat on. Just break one off, leaving around 20cm of stem, and wrap the stem with a leaf, or a cloth.

If you want to get much more elaborate, you can make all sorts of little figures with poppy heads, sweet corn stems and leaves.

Daisy chain

Find some daisies that have fairly long stems. Use your nail to make a vertical slit in the stem of one. Push the stem of a second daisy through this hole. Now make a slit in the stem of the second one, and push through the stem of a third, etc. You can create a chain by linking the first daisy to the last. Make it long enough to fit easily over the child's head.

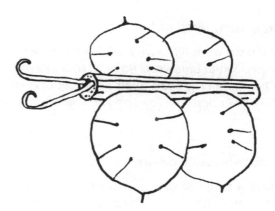

★ Hogweed may cause skin irritation in a few people.

Dragonfly

- *5-6cm hogweed (or other) stalk (see honesty butterfly)*
- *4 maple or sycamore tree seed wings*

Make slits in the corn stalk, and gently insert the wings so that they look like dragonfly wings.

Suzy, Suzy, jump out of bed!

When we were little, we'd pick the trumpet-shaped white bindweed flowers, squeeze the bottom and cry, 'Suzy, Suzy, jump out of bed!'. The flower pops off, leaving you with the green sepals.

A Midsummer crown

Make a ring out of a bunch of goose grass. Decorate with daisies, buttercups, or other flowers.

Daisies

Pull off the tiny petals, one by one, and they will tell you whether '...she loves me, she loves me not...' It can also be done with the seeds of couch grass, or extracting pips from an apple core:

> He loves me,   *He don't,*
> He'll have me,   *He won't,*
> He would if he could,   *But he can't*
> So he don't.

Yarrow arrow

Yarrow is common in hedgerows, gardens and rough places. It has a flexible ropy stalk. Find one that is flowering and tie a knot in the stalk. When you slide the knot up towards the head, it will shoot off like an arrow.

Clover honey

The narrow white and purple petals have a sweet tip at their base, which is sweet to suck.

Do you like butter?

Hold a buttercup flower under someone's chin and ask, 'Do you like butter?' If you can see a yellow reflection, they like it! See 'Buttercup' songs on page 45.

Four-leaf clover

Very occasionally, little beady eyes will find a cloverleaf with four segments rather than the usual three. It is very lucky!

Autumn

Welcome to you, rich Autumn days,
Ere comes the cold, leaf-picking wind.

W. H. DAVIES

Apples and fruits

*When we go walking, in the countryside, I love
to sing seasonal songs. It makes me feel good,
like we're noticing the changes. It feels like a
celebration that we're singing about it.*

Autumn is near

CD TRACK 56

WORDS AND MUSIC: CANDY VERNEY

Autumn is near, nights turning cold,

Black- berries in the hedge- rows and leaves red and gold.

Autumn is near,
Nights turning cold,
Blackberries in the hedgerows
And leaves red and gold.

Scythe the Wheat

Scythe the wheat, at its feet;   *(child jumps while you whisk an
                                   imaginary scythe under her feet)*
Bind it, bind it into bundles.   *(turn child round)*
Toss the wheat sheaves into the cart,   *(toss child gently onto sofa)*
Rickety rackety off it trundles!   *(clap twice on Rick and Rack)*
                                   NICOLA WICKSTEED

*A game for older children – some children are 'farmers', some are
'wheat'. Farmers imitate scything, wheat jumps; farmers turn the
wheat around; wheat jumps onto a sheet; farmers pull them along.*

Blackberries

CD TRACK 57

WORDS: NICOLA WICKSTEED   MUSIC: CANDY VERNEY

I have a basket; I'll tell you why, I'm picking blackberries to bake in a pie. I'll

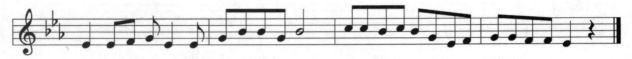

mix them with apple, put pastry on the top. If my pie is good enough, Don't buy one from the shop.

I have a basket;
I'll tell you why,
I'm picking blackberries
To bake in a pie.
I'll mix them with apple,
Put pastry on the top.
If my pie is good enough,
Don't buy one from the shop.

Yellow the bracken

WORDS: FLORENCE HOATSON   MUSIC: CANDY VERNEY

Yellow the bracken, golden the sheaves,   *(circle in a ring)*
Rosy the apples, crimson the leaves,
Mist on the hillside, clouds grey and white, *(one hand sweeps horizontally, the other stretches to clouds)*
Autumn good morning, summer good night. *(bow to autumn, hands together by cheek for summer)*

67

My nice red rosy apple

CD TRACK 59

WORDS: TRADITIONAL GERMAN

MUSIC: CANDY VERNEY

My nice red rosy apple has a secret all un- seen. If

you could peep in- side you'd see five rooms so neat and clean.

My nice red rosy apple
Has a secret all unseen.
If you could peep inside you'd see
Five rooms so neat and clean.

In each one is living
Two pips so black and bright.
Asleep they are and dreaming
Of lovely warm sunlight.

And sometimes they are dreaming
Of many things to be.
How soon they will be hanging
Upon the Christmas tree.

*If you cut an apple crossways, you clearly see
the five rooms.*

Hurry little children

WORDS AND MUSIC: ESTHER L. NELSON

Hurry little children, come a- long with me; come in- to the

garden and shake the apple tree. I will shake the big ones,

you can shake the small. When we've filled our basket,

slower

home we'll take them all, home we'll take them all.

Hurry little children, come along with me;   *(run round)*
Come into the garden and shake the apple tree.   *(mime)*
I will shake the big ones, you can shake the small.
When we've filled our basket,   *(gather up apples)*
Home we'll take them all,   *(stagger home)*
Home we'll take them all.

*Children will love to fill **your** basket.*

Rosy apple, mellow pear

CD TRACK 61

TRADITIONAL

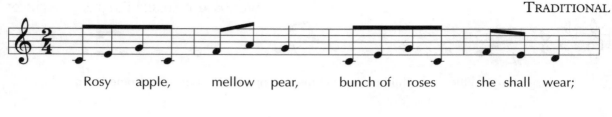

Rosy apple, mellow pear, bunch of roses she shall wear;

Gold and silver by her side; I know who will be my bride.

Rosy apple, mellow pear,
Bunch of roses she shall wear;
Gold and silver by her side;
I know who will be my bride.

Take her by the lily-white hand,
Lead her across the water,
Blow her a kiss and say goodbye;
She's the captain's daughter.

*A traditional English singing game. Children
form a circle and dance around. The child in the
middle of the ring chooses someone to be his
bride. Dance together in the centre, then another
child has a go.*

A dandling rhyme:

Catch him, crow! Carry him, kite!
Take him away till the apples are ripe;
When they are ripe and ready to fall,
Here comes baby, apples and all.

*We used to sing songs with the children that
connected with the seasons, about tumbling
leaves and bonfires, and sweeping etc. for
autumn. The children would learn these from
us, and then sing them for themselves as they
played outside amongst the leaves.*

We are walking

CD TRACK 62

WORDS: JULIE TONKIN   MUSIC: CANDY VERNEY

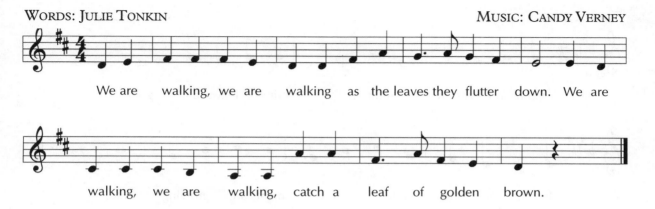

We are walking, we are walking as the leaves they flutter down. We are

walking, we are walking, catch a leaf of golden brown.

We are walking, we are walking
As the leaves they flutter down.
We are walking, we are walking
Catch a leaf of golden brown.

We are skipping, we are skipping
As the leaves they flutter down,
We are skipping, we are skipping
Catch a leaf of golden brown.

We are running, we are running
As the leaves they flutter down,
We are running, we are running
Catch a leaf of golden brown.

Make sure you sing this song with a rhythm that reflects the actions – i e. the Walking verse at a walking pace, the Skipping verse so that you can skip to it, (in a 6/8 rhythm), the Running verse at a running pace (as on CD).

You can add more verses of your own.

What do you suppose?

Oh what do you suppose?
What do you suppose?
In autumn when it's getting cold,
The trees take off their clothes.
                              NICOLA WICKSTEED

Crimson leaves in autumn

CD TRACK 63

WORDS: ANON.

MUSIC: CANDY VERNEY

Crimson leaves in autumn, crimson leaves and gold.
Berries for the little birds when nights are growing cold.

Fallen leaves in winter, branches brown and bare,
Bread for the little birds, as much as you can spare.

Autumn leaves

CD TRACK 64

WORDS: NICOLA WICKSTEED   MUSIC: CANDY VERNEY

Chestnut and sycamore, all shapes of leaves are falling down in the

autumn breeze: Oak leaves, ash leaves and hazel too. A-

long came the wind Phooooo! And a- way they blew.

A ring game:

Chestnut and sycamore,   *(hold hands in a ring, dance round)*
All shapes of leaves
Are falling down in the autumn breeze: *(bring hands to the ground)*
Oak leaves, ash leaves and hazel too.
Along came the wind
Phooooo!   *(blow)*
And away they blew.   *(children run to one corner altogether)*

Looking at a poppy seed head:

Proud poppy stands straight and tall,
Her tiny seeds are small so small;
Her crowned head shelters them inside
Till brother wind will scatter them wide!
Hear the rustle, hear the rustle... rustle...
CANDY VERNEY

73

Wind

CD TRACK 65

I am the wind

W<small>ORDS AND MUSIC</small>: E<small>LISABETH</small> L<small>EBRET</small>

I am the wind, I breeze and blow, m... m... , m... m... , listen, listen

how I whisper, m... m... , m... m... , in the tree, listen to me.

I am the wind, I breeze and blow,
m... m... , m... m... ,
Listen, listen how I whisper,
m... m... , m... m... ,
In the tree, listen to me.

The little winds they whisper
They whisper as they pass,
They tell their tiny secrets
To the flowers and the grass.
The big winds go a-buffeting,
A-blustering about.
The little winds whisper,
The big winds SHOUT.

ANON.

When the wind blows

CD TRACK 66

WORDS: TRADITIONAL

MUSIC: CANDY VERNEY

When the wind blows then the mill goes, when the wind drops then the mill stops:

fast   getting slower   and   stop

Clickety,   clackety,   clickety,   clackety,   clickety,   clackety,   clickety, clack.

When the wind blows   *(turn around, arms out)*
Then the mill goes,
When the wind drops   *(slow down)*
Then the mill stops:
Clickety, clackety, clickety, clackety,   *(tap on knees, slower and slower)*
Clickety, clackety, clickety, clack.

Leaves

Around we go, around we go, a-whirling in the wind,   *(twirl round)*
And down we go, and down we go to nestle on the ground.   *(crouch on floor)*

CANDY VERNEY

Animals

Lean Daddy Longlegs

CD TRACK 67

WORDS: ANON.

MUSIC: CANDY VERNEY

Lean Daddy Longlegs underneath a stone, have you any company, or are you a- lone?

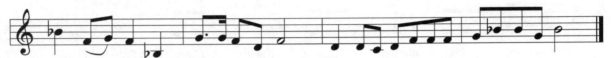

Peep, peep under, peep and you will see two spotted ladybirds are sitting here with me.

Lean Daddy Longlegs underneath a stone,
Have you any company, or are you alone?
Peep, peep under, peep and you will see
Two spotted ladybirds are sitting here with me.

Lean Daddy Longlegs underneath a stone,
Have you any company, or are you alone?
Peep, peep under, peep and you will see
Three beetles inky black are sitting here with me.

Lean Daddy Longlegs underneath a stone,
Have you any company, or are you alone?
Peep, peep under, peep and you will see
Six skinny earwigs are sitting here with me.

Lean Daddy Longlegs underneath a stone,
Have you any company, or are you alone?
Peep, peep under, peep and you will see
Four and twenty spiders are sitting here with me.

Lean Daddy Longlegs, pray what will you say
If children going home from school roll the stone away?
If children going home from school roll the stone away,
Then all my little guests and I must say Good-day!

Hop old squirrel

WORDS AND MUSIC: K. FORRAI

Hop old squirrel, eidledum, eidledum, hop old squirrel, eidledum, dee.

Hop old squirrel, eidledum, eidledum, hop old squirrel, eidledum, dee.

A hopping and jumping song

Hop old squirrel, eidledum, eidledum,
Hop old squirrel, eidledum, dee.
Hop old squirrel, eidledum, eidledum,
Hop old squirrel, eidledum, dee.

Hiding Hazelnuts

The squirrels gather hazelnuts
And hide them in the ground.
They hope that when they need a snack,
They'll easily be found.

There are some nuts that they forget.
It's likely some of these
Will turn into the seedlings which
Grow into hazel trees.

NICOLA WICKSTEED

My friend the squirrel

CD TRACK 69

WORDS: JULIE TONKIN   MUSIC: CANDY VERNEY

My friend the squirrel sits and stares, nose up high,

sniffing air, twitching here, twitching there.

My friend the squirrel sits and stares,
Nose up high, sniffing air,
Twitching here, twitching there.

My friend the squirrel puffs his cheek
Holds his nut, brown and sleek
Looks for tree-hole, takes a peek.

My friend the squirrel runs up tree
Jumps a branch – most nimbly
In his hibernation home to be.

Finger game

Four scarlet berries
Left upon the tree,   *(4 fingers)*
"Thanks," cried the blackbird,
"These will do for me."   *(other hand is a beak)*
He ate numbers one and two,
And then ate number three.   *(beak eats)*
When he'd eaten number four,
There was none to see!   *(open hands, empty)*

MARY VIVIAN

(see *The Singing Day* for more finger games)

Dark November days

– Halloween, Bonfire Night, Martinmas. These festivals bring light into the growing darkness. We cut out turnip or pumpkin lanterns and put them in the window. Children in many countries enjoy making paper lanterns at this time of year, and then how exciting it is to walk in the dark with a shining lantern under the stars (adult supervision required!).

(For instructions on how to make paper lanterns, see *Families, Festivals and Food*, reference in the Bibliography).

Pumpkin

CD TRACK 70

WORDS AND MUSIC: K. FORRAI

Pumpkin, pumpkin, round and fat, turn into a Jack-o-Lantern just like that.

Pumpkin, pumpkin, round and fat,
Turn into a Jack-o-Lantern just like that.

One child stands in front of the others with his back turned. On the last word of the song, he turns around and makes a frightening face.

Peter Peter pumpkin eater
Had a wife and couldn't keep her;
He put her in a pumpkin shell,
There he kept her very well.
TRADITIONAL

Six ghosts

TRADITIONAL

Six ghosts lurking in the shadow of the door,

Six ghosts lurking in the shadow of the door. But if

one should jump out at us, be ab - so - lute - ly sure there'd be

five ghosts lurking in the shadow of the door.

Six ghosts lurking in the shadow of the door,
Six ghosts lurking in the shadow of the door.
But if one should jump out at us, be absolutely sure
There'd be five ghosts in the shadow of the door.

Five ghosts lurking... etc.

Heave and heave-ho

CD TRACK 72

WORDS: JULIE TONKIN

MUSIC: ADAPTED BY CANDY VERNEY *

Drag the branches to the heap, to the heap, to the heap.

Drag the branches to the heap, heave and heave- ho.

Drag the branches to the heap,
To the heap, to the heap.
Drag the branches to the heap,
Heave and heave-ho.

Pile them high and stack them steep,
Stack them steep, stack them steep
Pile them high and stack them steep,
Heave and heave-ho.

Pack the spaces strong and firm,
Strong and firm, strong and firm,
Pack the spaces strong and firm,
Heave and heave-ho.

Stand well back, it's time to burn,
Time to burn, time to burn,
Stand well back, it's time to burn,
Heave and heave-ho.

Firework night

Who is drawing pictures on the black night sky?
Swirls of red and yellow up so high, so high?
Noisy cracks and bangs make the babies cry.
Who is drawing pictures on the black night sky?

JULIE TONKIN

* Adapted by Candy Verney from a
traditional song.

My bright little lantern

TRADITIONAL GERMAN

I go with my bright little lantern, my lantern is going with me. In Heaven the stars are shining, on Earth shines my lantern with me. The light grows dim as we go in, la-bimmel la-bimmel la-bim, bim, bim, the light grows dim as we go in, la-bimmel, la-bimmel, la-bim.

I go with my bright little lantern,
My lantern is going with me.
In Heaven the stars are shining,
On Earth shines my lantern with me.
The light grows dim as we go in,
La-bimmel la-bimmel la-bim, bim, bim,
The light grows dim as we go in,
La-bimmel, la-bimmel, la-bim.

Glimmer, lantern, glimmer

TRADITIONAL DUTCH

Glimmer, lantern, glimmer, little stars a- shim - mer,

O- ver rock and soil and stone, wander, trip- ping little gnome.

Pee- witt, pee- witt, tick- a- tick- a -tick, rou- cou, rou- cou.

Glimmer, lantern, glimmer,
Little stars a-shimmer,
Over rock and soil and stone,
Wander, tripping little gnome.
Pee-witt, pee-witt, tick-a-tick-a-tick,
Rou-cou, rou-cou.

Glimmer, Lantern glimmer
Little stars a-shimmer,
Over meadow moor and dale
Flitter flutter elfin veil,
Pee-witt, pee-witt, tick-a-tick-a-tick,
Rou-cou, rou-cou.

Autumn activities

See Introduction 'Singing and the Natural World', page x.

All plants listed have a particular interest for children.

TREES USEFUL ALL YEAR ROUND

I consider both willow and hazel as essential for any children's play area. They provide a valuable resource throughout the year.

Willow – *grows very fast, providing plenty of material for weaving, whittling, binding, making sticks, and other uses. It roots so easily that a piece of willow stuck in the ground will sprout a new plant. In this way you can grow your own stock and use it to make houses, tunnels and arbours.*

Hazel – *once it is established, will grow fast and provide a generous supply of strong, straight sticks and poles, which children will put to any number of uses.*

FRUIT AND NUT TREES TO GROW

Ask advice about varieties from a good local grower

For jams:
  Crab apple
  Rowanberry
  Damson
  Elderberry – *also makes a good cough medicine*

To eat from the tree:
  Plum
  Apple
  Hazelnut
  Pear
  And don't forget blackberries!

EASY-TO-GROW VEGETABLES
that are harvested in autumn

Pumpkin and squash: many varieties – *perfect for Halloween, and they will keep for several months.*

Tomatoes: *if the plants have not ripened before the bad weather sets in, pick the whole plant, and hang it inside. You will soon be able to pick fresh red tomatoes every day.*

Potatoes: *once the green plant starts to die off, dig it up and find the clean white potatoes hiding under the earth.*

SHRUBS FOR AUTUMN COLOUR

Smokebush – *Cotinus*

Spindle – *Euonymus europaeus 'Red Cascade': the seedpod is like a fiery flame when it bursts open. Poisonous*

Amelanchier

Ceratostigma

Virginia creeper – *Parthenocissus henryana (Chinese creeper) and P. thomsonii are both less vigorous varieties. P. quinquefolia is poisonous and an irritant*

Things to do in autumn

In parks and woods:

Fir cones, beechnut shells and acorns

Gather and use for play.

Sheep's wool

You can often find bits of sheep's wool hanging on wire fences or hedges where sheep have been. It makes ideal bedding or stuffing for dolls.

Ash tree 'keys'

Throw the seeds of the ash tree up in the air and watch how they twirl down.

Apple

Cut in half across, and see the rooms inside. See *My nice red rosy apple* on page 68.

Hedgerow jelly

A delicious jelly can be made using any fruits that you find in hedgerows or parks:

    blackberry
    apple
    hawthorn
    rowanberry
    elderberry
    sloe
    damson

and more (see *Family, Festivals and Food* – reference in the Bibliography).

Conker animals:

Use conkers joined together with toothpicks to make different animals.

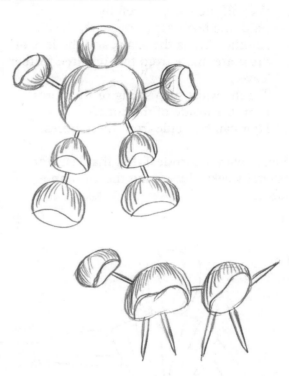

The conker game

This is a game our children used to love: the child plays the part of the chestnut and curls up on the floor. Adult plays the part of the weather in the different seasons, i.e, with flat of hand patting on the child's back as snow, fingertips on his back as rain, making wind with a scarf, rubbing his back for warm sun. Whilst this is happening, the child acts out roots going down into the ground then a tree growing upwards towards the sun, stretching out its branches, growing leaves etc. Then finally in the autumn again it becomes a conker fallen from the tree.

Corn dolls

You need some fresh sweet corn still covered
with leaves.

- Peel off the leaves carefully.
- Fold one leaf over to make the head.
- Another leaf is the arms, and the legs or
  dress are made from two or three further
  leaves.
- Tie the waist with string or the fibres
  from the inside of the corn.
- Hair can be made from these fibres.

Finish with a corn leaf doll that lasts for
several weeks, decorating the autumn
table.

Winter

Cold winter's in the wood
I saw him pass
Crinkling up fallen leaves
Along the grass.

EILEEN MATTHEWS

Winter weather

CD TRACK 75

Blow, north wind blow

WORDS AND MUSIC: CANDY VERNEY

Blow, north wind blow,   all the leaves are falling.   Cold frost and snow,   winter comes a- calling

Mother nature sleeps now,   all the earth is   bare.   Deep in the ground she hides her treasures rare.

Blow, north wind blow,   *(shake arms)*
All the leaves are falling.   *(wiggle fingers downwards)*
Cold frost and snow,   *(pretend to be cold)*
Winter comes a-calling.   *(beckon with arm)*
Mother nature sleeps now,   *(lie down)*
All the earth is bare.
Deep in the ground
She hides her treasures rare.   *(spread light cloth over child)*

Young children love being covered over with a cloth!

89

Hello Brother Wind

CD TRACK 76

WORDS: NICOLA WICKSTEED   MUSIC: CANDY VERNEY

Hello Brother Wind,   you can be a breeze,   or a hurly- burly   hurricane

Crashing through the trees.   You can be a sudden gust that   steals my hat with ease,

Or the gales   that whip up waves   on   the   seven   seas.

Hello Brother Wind, you can be a breeze,
Or a hurly-burly hurricane crashing through the trees.
You can be a sudden gust that steals my hat with ease,
Or the gales that whip up waves on the seven seas.

To watch a thunder storm and stop it being scary:

The thunder roared
The lightning flashed
And all the earth was shaken;
The little pig curled up his tail
and r...a...n to save his bacon.

TRADITIONAL

Start quiet and end loud and laughing

90

Blow, wind, blow!

ADAPTED BY CANDY VERNEY *

Blow, wind, blow! Drift the flying snow! Send it twirling, whirling over- head. There's a bedroom in a tree where as snug as snug can be, the squirrel nests with- in his cosy bed.

Blow, wind, blow!
Drift the flying snow!
Send it twirling, whirling overhead.
There's a bedroom in a tree
Where as snug as snug can be,
The squirrel nests within his cosy bed.

Shriek, wind, shriek,
Make the branches creak!
Battle with the boughs till break of day.
In a burrow warm and tight
Through the icy winter night
The rabbit sleeps the peaceful hours away.

Scold, wind, scold,
So bitter and so bold!
Whip around the hedgerows bare and strong.
Under holly, sloe and thorn,
In a set so soft and warm
Brock the badger sleeps the winter long.

* Adapted by Candy Verney from M. F.
Butts and Marlys Swinger

The north wind doth blow

TRADITIONAL

The north wind doth blow and we shall have snow and what will the robin do then poor thing? He'll

slow down

sit in the barn and keep himself warm, and hide his head under his wing, poor thing.

The north wind doth blow
And we shall have snow
And what will the robin do then poor thing?
He'll sit in the barn
And keep himself warm,
And hide his head under his wing, poor thing.

The north wind doth blow
And we shall have snow
And what will the swallow do then poor thing?
O, did you not know
He's gone long ago
To a country much warmer than ours.

The north wind doth blow
And we shall have snow
And what will the dormouse do then, poor thing,
Rolled up in a ball
In his nest snug and small,
He'll sleep till the winter is past.

The north wind doth blow
And we shall have snow,
And what will the children do then, poor things?
O, when nursery is done,
They'll jump, skip and run,
And play till they make themselves warm.

Little Robin Redbreast
Sat upon a rail;
Niddle noddle went his head,
Wiggle waggle went his tail.
                    TRADITIONAL

Puddle

CD TRACK 79

WORDS: NICOLA WICKSTEED   MUSIC: ARRANGED BY CANDY VERNEY *

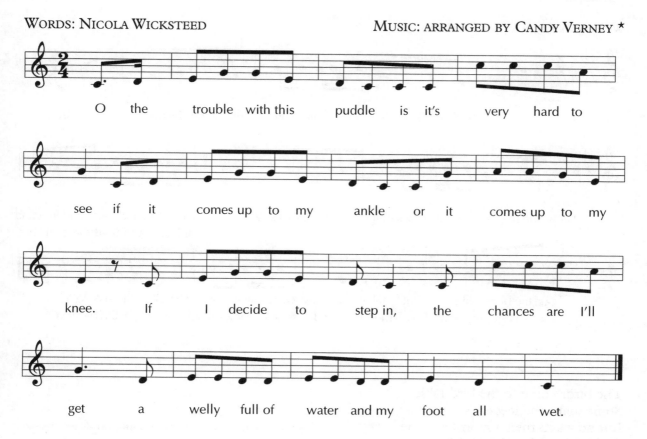

O the trouble with this puddle
Is it's very hard to see
If it comes up to my ankle
Or it comes up to my knee.
If I decide to step in,
The chances are I'll get
A welly full of water
And my foot all wet.

Doctor Foster went to Gloucester
In a shower of rain,
He stepped in a puddle right up to his middle
And never went there again.

TRADITIONAL

* Arranged by Candy Verney from a
traditional Scots tune.

Monster

WORDS: NICOLA WICKSTEED

MUSIC: CANDY VERNEY

The birds come to the bird table. Some make the feeders sway. But

now and then a monster comes AND CHASES THEM AWAY. I put out nuts and seeds and fruit and
only want to feed the birds but

hope the birds will stay. But still that monster comes along AND CHASES THEM A- WAY. I
I can't get my way. That monster called a squirrel comes AND CHASES THEM A- WAY.

The birds come to the bird table.
Some make the feeders sway.
But now and then a monster comes
AND CHASES THEM AWAY.

I put out nuts and seeds and fruit
And hope the birds will stay.
But still that monster comes along
AND CHASES THEM AWAY.

I only want to feed the birds
But I can't get my way.
That monster called a squirrel comes
AND CHASES THEM AWAY.

Birdies' breakfast

Two little birdies, one wintry day,
Began to wonder, and then to say,
'How about breakfast, this wintry day?'

Two little children, that wintry day,
Into the garden soon took their way,
Where the snow lay deep, that wintry day.

One with her broom swept the snow away;
One scattered crumbs, then went to play;
So the birdies had breakfast that wintry day.

ANON.

Rabbit

CD TRACK 81

WORDS AND MUSIC: K. FORRAI

Rabbit run on the frozen ground, who told you so?

Rabbit run on the frozen ground, how do you know?

I caught a rabbit uh-huh! I caught a rabbit uh-huh!

I caught a rabbit uh-huh! I caught a rabbit oh!

Rabbit run on the frozen ground,
Who told you so?
Rabbit run on the frozen ground,
How do you know?

Chorus:
I caught a rabbit uh-huh!
I caught a rabbit uh-huh!
I caught a rabbit uh-huh!
I caught a rabbit oh!

Foxy run on the frozen ground,
Who told you so?
Foxy run on the frozen ground,
How do you know?

Make up verses of your own, about other animals in winter.

King Winter is come

CD TRACK 82

WORDS: JULIE TONKIN

MUSIC: CANDY VERNEY

King   Win - ter   is   come   and   the   chill   winds   blow   his

crown   of   ice   and   his   cloak   of   snow.

King Winter is come
And the chill winds blow
His crown of ice
And his cloak of snow.

One child can dress as King Winter,
in a white cloth for his cloak, and a
silver crown. He can sit on his throne,
or walk around freezing everybody.

King Winter is strong
King Winter is bold,
King Winter is making the earth very cold
His beard is so long it goes down to the ground.
CANDY VERNEY

Mark your steps

WORDS: ANON.

MUSIC: CANDY VERNEY

Mark your steps with your feet on the white snow. Little holes, bigger holes, look where you go.

Mark your steps with your feet
On the white snow.
Little holes, bigger holes,
Look where you go.

Home Thoughts

When I'm out in the cold
And it's snowing or it's sleeting,
I'm glad to know at home
We've got a fire and central heating.

NICOLA WICKSTEED

*I always sing to my children when I am
frightened and need to be brave for them.
This usually happens when we're driving over
Dartmoor at night. The bad weather sets in,
and we feel muffled and isolated by the rain
and fog. We mostly sing well-known nursery
rhymes, but the more nervous I am the more
I choose jolly songs like 'Oh! A-hunting we will
go' (Singing Day, page 61) or 'Hot Cross Buns'
(Singing Year, page 13).*

Here is the woodcutter, sturdy and strong,
With an axe on his shoulder he strides along.
He chops the wood with a swing of his arm
Chop chop chop!
Branches fallen in winter storm
Chop chop chop!
And brings it home for the fire side warm
Tramp tramp tramp!

CANDY VERNEY

Children love to imitate the actions.

The Mitten Song

CD TRACK 84

WORDS: M. L. ALLEN

MUSIC: MARLYS SWINGER

Thumbs in the thumb-place, fingers all to- gether!   This is the song we   sing in mitten- weather.

When it is cold, it   doesn't matter whether   mittens are wool or   made of finest leather.

This is the song we sing in mitten- weather. Thumbs in the thumb-place, fingers all to- gether!

Thumbs in the thumb-place,
Fingers all together!
This is the song we sing in mitten-weather.
When it is cold, it doesn't matter whether
Mittens are wool or made of finest leather.
This is the song we sing in mitten-weather.
Thumbs in the thumb-place,
Fingers all together!

Let's put on our mittens
And button up our coat
Wrap a scarf snugly
Around our throat,
Pull on our boots
Fasten the straps
And tie on tightly
Our warm winter caps,
Then open the door,
And out we will go
Into the soft and feathery snow!

ANON.

In from the garden,
In from the snow
We take off our hats and coats and boots…
And by the fire we go.

CANDY VERNEY

Jeremiah, blow the fire,
Puff, puff, puff!
First you blow it gently,
Then you blow it rough.

TRADITIONAL

*Hold hands in a ring,
crouch down, pretending
the fire is in the middle.*

*Even at the slightest touch of white outside, Angus
comes running in, talking about Jack Frost.*

Jack Frost, what a sight!
Did you dance in the night,
Waggle your fingers, jump around
And scatter the frost all over the ground?

NICOLA WICKSTEED

Jack Frost is very small,
I'm sure he's out today.
He nipped my nose
And pinched my toes
When I went out to play.

ANON.

Look out! Look out!
Jack Frost is about!
He's after your fingers and toes;
And all through the night,
That gay little sprite
Is working where nobody knows.

He'll climb each tree,
So nimble is he,
His silvery powder he'll shake;
To windows he'll creep,
And while we're asleep,
Such wonderful pictures he'll make.

Across the grass
He'll merrily pass,
And change all its greenness to white;
Then home he will go
And laugh, "Ho! Ho! Ho!
What fun I have had in the night!"

CECILY E. PIKE

Festival traditions

*Many festivals around the world are based on a
lunar calendar. Consequently, the date they are
celebrated varies each year. Here are three
moveable festival songs from different traditions*

Divali

CD TRACK 85

Hari Krishna

TRADITIONAL

Hari Krish - na, Hari Krish - na Krishna

Krish - na Hari ha - ri.

Hari Krishna, Hari Krishna
Krishna Krishna Hari hari.

Hari Krishna, Hari Krishna
Krishna Krishna Hari hari.

Hari Rama, Rama Rama
Rama Rama Hari hari.

Hari Rama, Rama Rama
Rama Rama Hari hari.

*The moveable five day festival of Divali – the
Festival of Lights – is when Hindus celebrate
New Year, and Sikhs remember their sixth Guru,
Hargobind.*

*This song celebrates two of the Hindu gods,
Krishna and Rama. It is a Bhajan, in which the
leader sings a verse, then the group repeat it.
The song is sung as many times as wished,
usually getting faster and faster.*

Hanukkah

CD TRACK 86

Hanukkah is here

TRADITIONAL

One little candle burn burn burn, Ha - nuk - kah is here,

One little candle bright and clear, Ha - nuk - kah is here.

One little candle burn burn burn,
Hanukkah is here,
One little candle bright and clear,
Hanukkah is here,

Two little candles..... *(up to eight)*

The moveable Jewish festival of Hanukkah, also the Festival of Lights, commemorates the renewing of the Temple in Jerusalem in 164BC and the Temple's miraculous lamp.

Eid-Ul-Fitr

CD TRACK 87

Celebrate Eid

WORDS AND MUSIC: NANCY STEWART

Do you see   a   crescent   moon   Do you   see   a   crescent   moon

When you   see   a   crescent moon   We can   celebrate   Eid.   2. We'll

1. Do you see a crescent moon
Do you see a crescent moon
When you see a crescent moon
We can celebrate Eid

2. We'll have a party with our friends
We'll have a party with our friends
We'll have a party with our friends
And celebrate Eid

3. We'll decorate with lots of lights

4. We'll dress up in our brand new clothes

5. We'll eat our special food together

The great Muslim celebration of Eid-Ul-Fitr lasts for three days at the end of Ramadan. The date moves forward by about eleven days each year, so can happen in summer or winter.

The fast of Ramadan commemorates the time when the holy teachings of the Koran were first made known to the Prophet Mohammad. It ends on the morning after the new moon is seen in the sky. Children are told to watch out for the new moon. During Eid-Ul-Fitr, Muslims exchange gifts and cards, and visit friends.

Advent

Winter is dark

WORDS ADAPTED AND MUSIC BY CANDY VERNEY

Winter is dark yet each tiny spark

Brightens the way to Christmas day.

Winter is dark
Yet each tiny spark
Brightens the way to Christmas day.

Cold is the night
But each candle light
Brightens the way to Christmas day.

Stones in the earth
Await the new birth
And brighten the way to Christmas day.

All trees are bare
Yet holly stands there
And brightens the way to Christmas day.

Birds in the storm
Green ivy keeps them warm
And brightens the way to Christmas day.

Donkey shaggy and black
Carries Mary on his back
And brightens the way to Christmas day.

We sang this song during Advent, starting with one verse, then gradually adding another, day by day, as we got closer to Christmas. It gave a wonderful feeling of anticipation, and helped us focus on the real story of Christmas, rather than the commercial build up. The children helped make up new verses.

During the first week we sang verses with reference to the mineral world, second week – plant world, third – animal world, fourth – human world.

Quiet all around

WORDS: M. E. VAN EBBENHORST TENGBERGEN   MUSIC: TRADITIONAL DUTCH

Quiet, quiet, quiet all a- round Listen, listen, don't make any sound. A

wonder's rustling softly here Jesus Christ is coming near Quiet, quiet, quiet all a- round.

Quiet, quiet, quiet all around
Listen, listen, don't make any sound.
A wonder's rustling softly here
Jesus Christ is coming near
Quiet, quiet, quiet all around.

Christmas

Christmas is coming and the geese are getting fat
Please put a penny in the old man's hat
Of you haven't got a penny, a ha'penny will do
If you haven't got a ha'penny, God bless you!

TRADITIONAL

For the twelve days of Christmas, we sing the carol 'The Twelve Days of Christmas', adding one verse each day.

Christmas comes but once a year
And when it does it brings good cheer,
And a pocketful of money, and a cellar full of beer,
And a good fat pig to last you all year.

TRADITIONAL

Children's Song of the Nativity

CD TRACK 89A

WORDS: FRANCES CHESTERTON   MUSIC: TRADITIONAL

How far is it to Beth- le- hem? Not very

far. Shall we find the stable room, lit by a

star? Can we see the little child, is he with- in? If

we lift the wooden latch, may we go in?

How far is it to Bethlehem?
Not very far.
Shall we find the stable room
Lit by a star?

Can we see the little child,
Is he within?
If we lift the wooden latch
May we go in?

May we stroke the creatures there,
Ox, ass, or sheep?
May we peep like them and see
Jesus asleep?

If we touch his tiny hand
Will he awake?
Will he know we've come so far
Just for his sake?

Great kings have precious gifts,
And we have naught,
Little smiles and little tears
Are all we have brought.

For all weary children
Mary must weep.
Here, on his bed of straw
Sleep, children, sleep.

God in his mother's arms,
Babes in the byre,
Sleep, as they sleep who find
Their heart's desire.

The Friendly Beasts

OLD ENGLISH CAROL

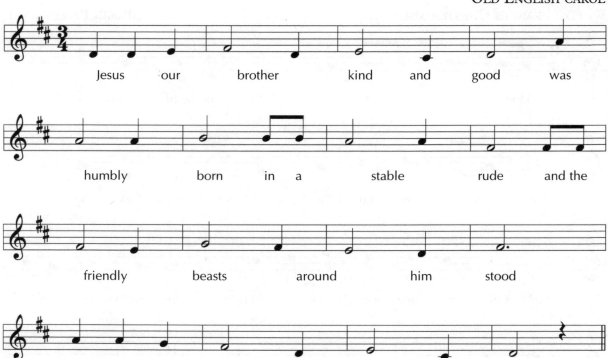

Jesus our brother kind and good
Was humbly born in a stable rude
And the friendly beasts around him stood
Jesus our brother, kind and good.

I said the donkey, all shaggy and brown,
I carried his mother up hill and down
I carried his mother to Bethlehem town.
I said the donkey, all shaggy and brown.

I said the cow, all white and red
I gave him my manger for his bed
I gave him my hay to pillow his head.
I said the cow, all white and red.

I said the sheep, with curly horn,
I gave him my wool for a blanket warm
He wore my coat on Christmas morn.
I said the sheep, with curly horn.

I said the dove from the rafters high.
I cooed him to sleep so he would not cry,
We cooed him to sleep, my mate and I.
I said the dove from the rafters high.

Thus every beast, by some good spell
In the stable rude was glad to tell
Of the gift he gave Emmanuel.
The gift he gave Emmanuel.

New Year

Today is Hogmanay

TRADITIONAL SCOTTISH

To- day is Hog-ma- nay To- morrow's Hogma- na-nay and

I'm going up the brae to see may ain wee Granny.

Today is Hogmanay
Tomorrow's Hogmananay
And I'm going up the brae
To see may ain wee Granny.

I'll tak' her tae a ball
I'll tak' her for a supper
And when I get her there
I'll stick her nose in the butter

Singin' a-a-a-a-a
a-a-a-a-a-a
a-a-a-a-a
And that's the Heilan' chorus.

God be here, God be there
We wish you all a happy new year;
God without, God within,
Let the Old Year out and the New Year in.
TRADITIONAL

Hogmanay – *New Year's Eve*
brae – *hill*
ain wee – *own small*
tae – *to*
Heilan' – *Highland*

Epiphany

CD TRACK 91A

Kings from faraway lands

WORDS AND MUSIC: ANON.

Kings from faraway lands we are Caspar, Melchior, Balthazar.

Star of Bethlehem, light of Bethlehem guide our wandering, golden star.

Kings from faraway lands we are
Caspar, Melchior, Balthazar.
Star of Bethlehem, light of Bethlehem
Guide our wandering, golden star.

Shining star

CD TRACK 91B

WORDS: JULIE TONKIN

MUSIC: CANDY VERNEY

Tell me a story shining star
Tell me where you've been,
Travelling both near and far
Places that you've seen.

Sing me a song oh winter star
Sing it loud and true
Lullaby my listening ear
Duet for me and you.

Snow

CD TRACK 92A

Frosty weather

WORDS AND MUSIC: K. FORRAI

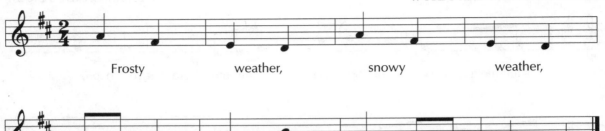

Frosty weather, snowy weather,

When the wind blows we all go to- gether!

Winter ring game

Frosty weather, snowy weather, *join hands in a circle and walk around.*
When the wind blows we all go together! *come together in the middle*

CD TRACK 92B

We gnomes walk in a row

WORDS AND MUSIC: ANON.

Ho ho ho, we gnomes walk in a row. Ho ho ho, we

gnomes walk in a row. Ho ho ho, we gnomes walk in a row.

Ho ho ho, we gnomes walk in a row.
Ho ho ho, we gnomes walk in a row.
Ho ho ho, we gnomes walk in a row.

Can be changed to
Ho ho ho, three (four, five) snowmen walk
in a row.

Good for walks, and can be sung in a round.

Little flakes of snow

TRADITIONAL GERMAN

O where do you come from you little flakes of snow, falling,

falling, softly falling on the earth below?

O where do you come from
You little flakes of snow,
Falling, falling, softly falling
On the earth below?

On the trees and on the bushes
On the mountains afar,
Tell me snowflakes do you come from
Where the angels are?

Snow, snow faster,
Ally-ally-baster;
The old woman's plucking her geese,
Selling the feathers a penny a-piece.
TRADITIONAL

Finger game

This is snowflakes playing about
Up in Cloudland they dance in and out.

This is how they whirl down the street
Powdering everybody they meet.

This is how they come fluttering down
Whitening the roads, the fields and the town.

This is how snowflakes cover the trees
Each branch and twig bends in the breeze.

This is how they cover the ground
Cover it thickly with never a sound.

This is how snowflakes blow in a heap
Looking just like fleecy sheep.

This is how people shiver and shake
On a sunny morning when they first awake.

This is how snowflakes melt away
When the sun sends out his beams to play.
ANON.

Ten little snowmen

CD TRACK 93B

WORDS AND MUSIC: ANON.

There were ten little snowmen, each with a scarf and a woolly hat. The sun came out and melted one, it's sad but that was that.

A circle game

There were ten little snowmen,
Each with a scarf and a woolly hat.
The sun came out and melted one,
It's sad but that was that.

There were nine little snowmen...etc.

There were no little snowmen,
Just scarves and woolly hats,
Sitting in a muddle in a very wet puddle,
It's sad but that was that.

Stuck in the snow

We've got a brilliant car.
It really likes to go,
But it's not going anywhere.
We're stuck in the snow.

It only got this far,
And now it needs a tow.
I hope the tractor comes along.
We're stuck in the snow.

Mum's got a mobile phone.
She's calling Uncle Joe.
I'm glad he drives a snow plough 'cos
We're stuck in the snow.

NICOLA WICKSTEED

Up in the morning

WORDS: ROBERT BURNS

MUSIC: TRADITIONAL SCOTS

Up in the morning's no for me
Up in the morning early
When a' the hills are covered wi' snaw
I'm sure it's winter fairly.

Winter tell us little bulbs
To tuck our heads in so.
Then we will not need to shiver
When the cold winds blow.

Spring will come with sun and showers,
Soon to raise our head,
Then we'll grow and grow and grow
Right out of bed.

ANON.

*Children love it if you tuck them up in a
light cloth for the first verse, then they sit
up when spring comes.*

Little town

WORDS: JULIE TONKIN   MUSIC: CANDY VERNEY

Little town how white you are, how cold and icy too. And all the rooftops

All around are white with snow a- new. Crunch go my big red boots and

slide go my feet, slipping slipping everywhere un- til the ground I meet!

Little town
How white you are,
How cold and icy too.
And all the rooftops
All around
Are white with snow anew.

Crunch go my big red boots
And slide go my feet,
Slipping slipping everywhere
Until the ground I meet!

High hill
How white you are
How cold and icy too
And all the gateposts
All around
Are white with snow anew.

Crunch go my big red boots
And slide go my feet
Slipping slipping everywhere
Until the ground I meet!

Make up more verses of your own!

Candlemas

CD TRACK 95A

Dipping candles song

WORDS AND MUSIC: CANDY VERNEY

Around and around and around and around, we dip our candles in the big old tin, and wait a little bit for it to drip drop in. We'll make e- nough to last the year to give us light and bring good cheer.

Around and around and around and around,
We dip our candles in the big old tin,
And wait a little bit for it to drip drop in.
We'll make enough to last the year
To give us light and bring good cheer.

Fade ...

This is a song for hand dipping candles. The hot melted wax is on the table, in a large old tin. Everyone has a wick which they dip in the hot melted wax. They walk around the table singing the song. By the time they have reached the tin again, their candle has cooled down enough to make another dipping.

Chinese New Year

CD TRACK 95B

Gung Hay Fat Choy

WORDS AND MUSIC: NANCY STEWART

Gung Hay Fat Choy   Gung Hay Fat Choy

Sing Happy New Year,   Gung Hay Fat Choy

The new year tells us,   ex- act- ly when

to ce- le- brate with   fa- mi- ly and friends.

Chorus:
Gung Hay Fat Choy   *clap in rhythm*
Gung Hay Fat Choy
Sing Happy New Year,
Gung Hay Fat Choy

The date of the Chinese New Year is based on the Chinese Lunar calendar and falls between mid-January to mid-February. Each year is given the name of one of the twelve animals associated with Buddha, and Chinese Astrology. The celebrations typically last for two weeks.

1. The new year tells us, exactly when   *(hold up one hand in C shape for moon)*
To celebrate with family and friends.

2. Clean up the house, get out the broom   *(pretend to sweep)*
Sweep out the old year, bring in the new.

3. The dragon dances, the lanterns light   *(hands together, and snake around)*
The firecrackers light up the night.   *(imitate fireworks: alternate arms shoot up with fingers opening)*

116

Winter activities

See Introduction 'Singing and the Natural World', page x.

All plants listed have a particular interest for children.

Plants to grow for winter scent and blossom

Daphne mezereum, Daphne odora – *poisonous*
Winter jasmine – *Jasminum nudiflorum*
Prunus subhirtella autumnalis
Viburnum bodnantense
Mahonia – *not only does this have fine-scented flowers, but children like to gently peel off bits of the bright yellow bark. Just watch out for the very spiky leaves*

Plants useful for Advent wreaths and Christmas decorations

Fir tree branches
Holly berries and branches
Pyracantha berries – *beware spikes*
Cotoneaster berries
Ivy – *poisonous and irritant*
Larch cones

Plants to attract winter birds

Ivy – *provides wonderful shelter for birds*
Pyracantha
Cotoneaster
Holly

Seed heads

Fennel
Teasel – *goldfinches will feed on the seeds*
Sedum
Lemon balm
Evening primrose
Poppy

Things to do in winter

Christmas decorations

Fir cones sprayed gold or silver look lovely on the Christmas tree.

Christmas mobile

Spray a branch of fir or larch with gold or silver. Hang it up somewhere, and attach decorations to it, making sure they hang at different levels. A candle lit below (make sure it is well away from the branch) will cause the whole mobile to turn gently.

Paper Whites

Narcissus 'Paper White' bulbs, planted in a pot in the autumn, will come up and flower by Christmas. They fill the house with the sweetest of scents.

Toothpick animals

Use tooth picks to make animals, with satsumas or corks for the body.

Walnut shell boats

Carefully split a walnut in two, take out the nut. Fill shell with candle wax and set a birthday candle in it. It will gently float in bowl of water. This is a magical centre-piece for a birthday party, too.

Songs for Every Season

Tozie Mozie

TRADITIONAL FROM ORKNEY

Come to the wood, says Tozie Mozie Come to the wood, says Johnnie Red- ho- sie,

Come to the wood, says brithers and three, Come to the wood, says Wise Willee.

Come to the wood, says Tozie Mozie
Come to the wood, says Johnnie Red-hosie,
Come to the wood, says brithers and three,
Come to the wood, says Wise Willee.

What to do there? says Tozie Mozie
What to do there? says Johnnie Red-hosie
What to do there? says brithers and three,
What to do there? says Wise Willee

The above two verses are part of a traditional song from Orkney, called *Hunting the Wren*. (A version from Oxfordshire is called *The Cutty Wren*). It can be adapted to any situation you find yourself in. Just keep to the same format. Here are some examples:

I've found some mushrooms, says Tozie Mozie etc.

But we won't pick them, says Tozie Mozie etc.

Look at the snowdrops, says Tozie Mozie etc.

I've found some conkers, says Tozie Mozie etc.

Let's go to town, says Tozie Mozie etc.

I tried Tozie Mozie in my nursery class with a difficult boy who was hitting others and refusing to clear up. He loves music and the effect was miraculous. He made up a verse of his own: 'We'll clear up the square ones, said Tozie Mozie'. Eventually he was holding up different shapes to see what the next verse would be.

What shall we do

WORDS AND MUSIC: K. FORRAI

What shall we do when we all go out, all go out, all go out,

What shall we do when we all go out, when we all go out to play?

Ring game

What shall we do when we all go out,
All go out, all go out,
What shall we do when we all go out
When we all go out to play?

Hold hands and walk round in a circle.
One child acts out the activity in the middle.

Here we go round the mountain

CD TRACK 97A

TRADITIONAL AMERICAN

Here we go round the mountain two by two,

Here we go round the mountain two by two,

Here we go round the mountain two by two,

Rise, su- gar, rise.

Here we go round the mountain two by two,
Here we go round the mountain two by two,
Here we go round the mountain two by two,
Rise, sugar, rise.

Make up other verses, e.g.
Here we go up the high street two by two
Here we go to the market two by two

Charlie over the ocean

CD TRACK 97B

WORDS AND MUSIC: K. FORRAI

Charlie over the o- cean   Charlie over the sea

Charlie caught a   blackbird,   Can't   catch   me.

Charlie over the ocean
> *Charlie over the ocean*
Charlie over the sea
> *Charlie over the sea*
Charlie caught a blackbird,
> *Charlie caught a blackbird,*
Can't catch me.
> *Can't catch me.*

There once was a mother

CD TRACK 98A

TRADITIONAL GERMAN

There once was a mother
With four little children
Called spring and summer
And autumn and winter.

Spring dances with flowers,
Summer shines with golden glow;
Autumn blesses with soft rain,
And winter sends snow.

May there always be sunshine

CD TRACK 98B

WORDS: TRADITIONAL RUSSIAN   MUSIC: CANDY VERNEY

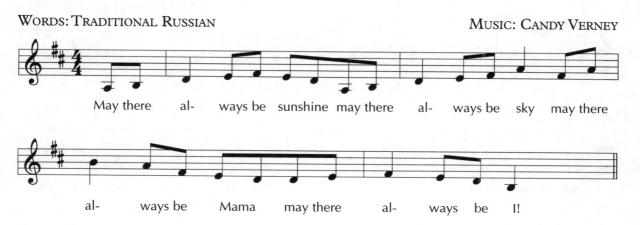

May there always be sunshine
May there always be sky
May there always be Mama
May there always be I!

*A Russian children's poem celebrating the
important things in life.*

Glory be to God

CD TRACK 99

WORDS AND MUSIC: CANDY VERNEY

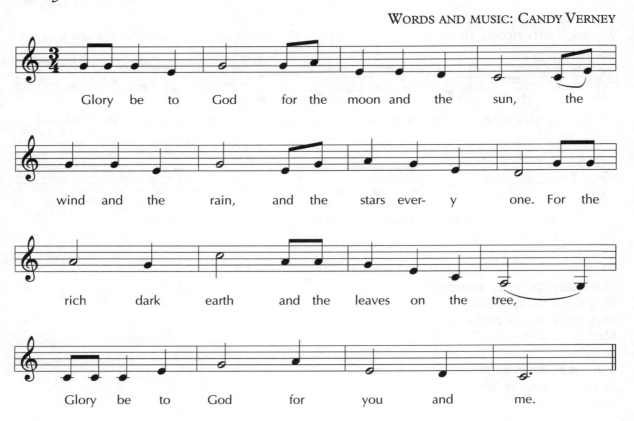

Glory be to God for the moon and the sun,
The wind and the rain, and the stars every one.
For the rich dark earth and the leaves on the tree,
Glory be to God for you and me.

Bibliography, sources and useful addresses

Songs by Candy Verney

(music unless specified otherwise)

Spring:
  Snowdrop down
  Spring gone shy
  Waiting for leaves
  Wake up!
  Catkins
  Pancake Tuesday
  The bird's nest (adapted)
  Little bird
  Little red robin (words and music)
  Chook chook
  My pigeon house
  Little hare
  Dot to frog
  Rain on the green grass
  Hippety hop
  The swing (words adapted)
  See-saw Sacradown

Summer:
  I'm busy busy busy said the bee (words and music)
  Butterfly (music arranged, and words)
  Swifts and swallows and martins
  Chicka chicka
  Buttercups
  Tomorrow is Midsummer's Day (words and music)
  Midsummer's Day (music arranged)
  Raspberries hide
  Pebbles
  Hearken in my tiny ear
  The kayak song
  Climbing a rock
  Shrimping

Autumn:
  Autumn is near (words and music)
  Blackberries
  Yellow the bracken
  My nice red rosy apple
  We are walking
  Crimson leaves in autumn
  Autumn leaves
  Lean Daddy Longlegs
  When the wind blows
  My friend the squirrel
  Heave and heave-ho (music adapted)

Winter:
  Blow, north wind blow (words and music)
  Hello Brother Wind
  Blow, wind, blow! (adapted)
  Puddle (music arranged)
  Monster
  King Winter is come
  Mark your steps
  Winter is dark (words adapted, and music)
  Shining star
  Little town
  Dipping Candles song (words and tune)

Songs for Every Season:
  May there always be sunshine
  Glory be to God (words and music)

Poems by Candy Verney

Proud poppy
King Winter is strong
Leaves
The woodcutter
In from the garden

Poems by Nicola Wicksteed

Nicola lives in the Lake District where she assists her brother, a single dad, with the care of his little boy Michael. A writer of comic verse, light verse and lyrics, Nicola has had poems published in various magazines.

Michael has helped to inspire the verses included in this collection.

Spring:
- Spring gone shy
- Waiting for leaves
- The seed
- Wake up!
- Catkins
- Little bird
- The digger
- Caterpillar
- Dot to frog
- Frog
- Spring lambs
- The carpet
- Foxgloves

Summer:
- Oh no!
- Barn owl
- Swifts and swallows and martins
- Chicka chicka
- Midsummer's Day is a royal day
- Long days
- Robert Rabbit
- Raspberries hide
- Buckets and spades

Autumn:
- Scythe the wheat
- Blackberries
- What do you suppose?
- Autumn leaves
- Hiding hazelnuts

Winter:
- Hello Brother Wind
- Puddle
- Monster
- Home thoughts
- Jack Frost
- Stuck in the snow

Poems by Julie Tonkin

For Julie, the changing of the seasons was an essential part of growing up in the far west of Cornwall – surrounded by sea, country and rugged landscape. Julie is a trained special needs and adult literacy teacher. She is also mother to Teän, age 8, and Dominic, age 5, on whom she trials her writing for children. Julie has been a member of Candy Verney's Bradford on Avon community choir for five years.

Spring:
- In my oaken mossy root
- One woolly lamb's tail
- Woodpecker
- Creeping, creeping

Summer:
- Hearken in my tiny ear
- Jumping waves
- Climbing a rock
- Shrimping

Autumn:
- We are walking
- My friend the squirrel
- Heave and heave-ho
- Firework night

Winter:
- King Winter is come
- Shining star
- Little town

All other songs in the book, except for those whose origins could not be traced, are either included in the publications listed or are in the public domain as well-known songs.

Music books/sources

Carey, Diana and Large, Judy: *Festivals, Family and Food*, Hawthorn Press, 1982
Cass-Beggs, Barbara: *A Musical Calendar of Festivals*, Ward Lock Educational, 1983
Karpeles, Maud (ed): *Folk Songs of Europe*, Oak Publications, 1956
Karpeles, Maud (ed): *Oxford Book of Carols*, OUP, 1964
Lebret, Elisabeth: *Pentatonic Songs*, Waldorf Association of Ontario, 1985
Matterson, Elizabeth: *This little Puffin*, Puffin Books, 1991
Nelson, Esther L: *Singing and Dancing Games for the Very Young*, Sterling Publishing Company, NY, 1982
Opie, Iona & Peter: *Children's games in street and playground*, OUP, 1969
Opie, Iona & Peter: *The Oxford Book of Nursery Rhymes*, OUP, 1951
Opie, Iona & Peter: *The Oxford Nursery Rhyme Book*, OUP, 1955
Opie, Iona & Peter: *The Puffin Book of Nursery Rhymes*, Penguin Books, 1963
Opie, Iona & Peter: *The Singing Game*, OUP, 1985
Roberts, Sheena: *Playsongs*, Macdonald, 2000
Sandor, Frigyes (ed): *Music Education in Hungary*, Boosey & Hawkes and Corvina Press, 1975
Swinger, Marlys: *Sing through the Day*, Plough Publishing House, NY, 1968
Swinger, Marlys: *Sing through the Seasons*, Plough Publishing House, NY, 1972
Verney, Candy: *The Singing Day*, Hawthorn Press, 2003

Music books: no author/editor cited

Strawberry Fair, A & C Black Ltd, 1985
Spring Collection of Poems, Songs and Stories for young children, Wynstones Press, 1999
Summer Collection of Poems, Songs and Stories for young children, Wynstones Press, 1999
Autumn Collection of Poems, Songs and Stories for young children, Wynstones Press, 1999
Winter Collection of Poems, Songs and Stories for young children, Wynstones Press, 1999
Gateways: Poems, Songs and Stories for young children, Wynstones Press, 1999

Other Books

Al-Gailani, Noorah and Smith, Chris: *The Islamic Year*, Hawthorn Press, 2002
Campbell, Patricia Shehan: *Songs in their Heads, Music and its meaning in children's lives*, OUP, 1998
Forrai, Katalin: *Music in Preschool*, Corvina Press, 1990
Marshall, Ruth: *Celebrating Irish Festivals*, Hawthorn Press, 2003
McClellan, Randall: *The Healing Forces of Music*, Amity House, NY, 1988
Oldfield, Lynne: *Free To Learn*, Hawthorn Press, 2001
Raven, Michael (ed): *One Thousand English Country Dance Tunes*, Michael Raven, 1983
Rawson, Martyn, and Rose, Michael: *Ready To Learn*, Hawthorn Press, 2006
Sandor, Frigyes (ed): *Music Education in Hungary*, Boosey & Hawkes and Corvina Press, 1975
Stewart, Bob: *Where is Saint George?* Blandford Press, 1988
Thomas, Heather (ed): *Journey through time in Verse and Rhyme*, Rudolf Steiner Press, 1987
Book of a Thousand Poems, Collins Educational, 1972 (no editor cited)

Articles

Deliege: 'Musical Beginnings', OUP, 1996
Goddard Blythe, Sally: 'Music and Movement – Are these the lost keys to early learning?' Paper presented at the 10th European Conference of Neuro-Development Delay in Children with Specific Learning Difficulties, Chester 6-8 March 1998
Heather, Simon: 'The Healing Power of Sound', *Positive Health,* May 2001
Papousek, H. and Papousek. M: 'Intuitive Parenting' in: Osovsky Wiley, J.D (ed.), *Handbook of Infant Development,* New York 1987
Lindenberg, Christof-Andreas: 'The Child and Hearing': 3 articles in *The Cresset,* Camphill Publication, Vol 17 nos.2, 3, 4: 1971

Websites

- Children's Music by Nancy Stewart, Animal Crackers/Friends Street Music, 6505 SE 28th Street, Mercer Island, WA 98040, USA, **www.nancymusic.com**

- School of Scottish Studies Archive, **www.pearl.arts.ed.ac.uk**

- Topic Records Ltd, The Voice of the People series, **www.topicrecords.co.uk**

- 'The Power of Music' – worldwide literature review of authoritative articles which address the power of music, **www.thepowerofmusic.co.uk**

- 'Wired for Sound: The Essential Connection between Music and Development' by Cynthia Ensign Baney, **www.gymboreeplayuk.com/CATresearch.htm**

- International Kodaly Society, **www.iks.hu**

- British Kodaly Academy, **www.britishkodalyacademy.org**

- Organization of American Kodaly Educators, **www.oake.org**

- Steiner Waldorf Schools Fellowship, **www.steinerwaldorf.org.uk**

Organisations

- Singing in the Round
  Candy Verney offers regular and one-off workshops for pre-school children, parents and teachers. Her other work includes the popular Singing in the Round community choirs in Bath and Wiltshire, weekend workshops that combine singing with Landscape and Art, and courses for Bild-Werk in Frauenau, Germany. She also helps organise 'Singing Round the Town', a unique annual summer community festival in Bradford on Avon.
  Tel: (++44) (0) 1225 867366 E-mail: candyverney@hotmail.com
  www.candyverney.co.uk
  www.singingintheround.co.uk

- The Natural Voice Practitioners' Network.
  An organisation for voice teachers sharing a common ethos and approach to voice and song work. 'We believe that singing is everyone's birthright and we are committed to teaching styles that are accepting and inclusive of all, regardless of musical experience and ability.' For information about: voice teachers; singing workshops; community choirs; recordings and song resources; voice events in your area, throughout the UK and beyond contact:
  www.naturalvoice.net

- The Voices Foundation
  Suite 2, Ground floor, 38 Ebury Street, London SW1 W OLU
  Tel: (++44) (0)20 7730 6677 E-mail: vf@voices.org.uk
  www.voices.org.uk

- The Listening Centre (Lewes) Ltd – Tomatis
  Maltings Studio, 16A Station Street, Lewes, East Sussex BN7 2DB
  Tel: (++44) (0)1273 474877 E-mail: enquiries@listeningcentre.co.uk
  www.listeningcentre.co.uk
  www.tomatis.com

- Caroline Price, Community Choir Leader
  Stream of Sound, 24 Cleveland Street, Stourbridge, West Midlands DY8 3UE
  Tel: (++44) (0)1384 377833
  www.streamofsound.co.uk

- Tonalis Music Centre
  4 Castle Farm Close, Leighterton, Gloucestershire GL8 8UY
  Tel/Fax: (++44) (0)1666 890460 E-mail: tonalis@aol.com
  Tonalis offers weekend workshops, courses and trainings in Music Education, Voicework and Community Musicing. Some of the themes which Tonalis works with are Children's Musical Development – a new developmental music curriculum, Teaching Music through Movement, Sharing Music – how social ideals can inspire music in schools and Newly Designed Instruments for meeting children's needs etc.
  www.tonalismusic.co.uk

Music index of first lines

Music index of first lines

CD track numbers – list of first lines

1	Snowdrop down, crocus up	56	Autumn is near
2	It's supposed to be spring	57	I have a basket
3	The snowdrops are out	58	Yellow the bracken, golden the sheaves
4	Wake up, wake up, all you little children	59	My nice red rosy apple
5	I'm a dormouse	60	Hurry little children, come along with me
6	I love catkins	61	Rosy apple, mellow pear
7	Look who's here, it's Lady Spring	62	We are walking, we are walking
8	Lily, Lily Wallflowers	63	Crimson leaves in autumn
9	Shrove Tuesday, Ash Wednesday	64	Chestnut and sycamore
10	Pancake Tuesday, Mother's busy baking	65	I am the wind, I breeze and blow
11	Hot cross buns	66	When the wind blows
12	The winter now is over	67	Lean Daddy Longlegs underneath a stone
13	Cuckoo, cuckoo, messenger clear	68	Hop old squirrel, eidledum, eidledum
14	A little bird built a warm nest in a tree	69	My friend the squirrel sits and stares
15	Little bird make your nest	70	Pumpkin, pumpkin, round and fat
16	Little red robin up in a tree	71	Six ghosts lurking in the shadow of the door
17	Hear the blackbird sing	72	Drag the branches to the heap
18	Chook chook chook chook chook	73	I go with my bright little lantern
19	My pigeon house I open wide	74	Glimmer, lantern, glimmer
20	Dilly dilly duck	75	Blow, north wind blow
21	Creeping, creeping long the twig	76	Hello Brother Wind
22	See the little hare is fast asleep	77	Blow, wind, blow
23	Wriggledy wriggledy	78	The north wind doth blow
24	Nanny goat, Billy goat	79	O the trouble with this puddle
25	Here's a branch of snowy may	80	The birds come to the bird table
26	While walking in the woods one day	81	Rabbit run on the frozen ground
27	In and out the dusky bluebells	82	King Winter is come
28	Rain on the green grass	83	Mark your steps with your feet
29	Spring-time goodbye	84	Thumbs in the thumb-place
30	Hippety hop to the barber's shop	85	Hari Krishna, Hari Krishna
31	Now so high, now so low	86	One little candle burn burn burn
32	See-saw, Margery Daw	87	Do you see a crescent moon
33	See-saw, sacradown	88A	Winter is dark
34	I'm busy, busy, busy, said the bee	88B	Quiet, quiet, quiet all around
35	See the little butterfly	89A	How far is it to Bethlehem
36	Four and twenty tailors	89B	Jesus our brother kind and good
37	Swifts and swallows and martins	90	Today is Hogmanay
38	Chicka chicka, chicka chicka	91A	Kings from faraway lands we are
39	Over in the meadow, in the sand, in the sun	91B	Tell me a story shining star
40	Buttercups golden and gay	92A	Frosty weather, snowy weather
41	All around the buttercup	92B	Ho ho ho, we gnomes walk in a row
42	Lavender's blue, dilly dilly	93A	O where do you come from
43	Here we come a-haying	93B	There were ten little snowmen
44	Tomorrow is Midsummer's Day	94A	Up in the morning's no for me
45	Midsummer's Day is a royal day	94B	Little town how white you are
46	Shadows go round	95A	Around and around
47	I pick up me hoe an' I go	95B	Gung Hay Fat Choy
48	Savez-vous planter les choux	96A	Come to the wood, says Tozie Mozie
49	Old Mister Rabbit, you've got a mighty habit	96B	What shall we do when we all go out
50	Raspberries hide	97A	Here we go round the mountain two by two
51	Pebbles, pebbles, pebbles	97B	Charlie over the ocean
52	Hearken in my tiny ear	98A	There once was a mother
53	Over the dark water	98B	May there always be sunshine
54	Sun warmed shiny rock	99	Glory be to God for the moon and the sun
55	In the middle of my pool		

About the author

Candy Verney studied music at the University of Bristol, however most of her skills were learnt bringing up three sons, cultivating a garden and teaching music to all ages from the very young to the very old. She draws her inspiration from teaching methods used in Steiner/Waldorf education. Candy runs workshops with parents, teachers and toddlers. This is the companion volume to her first book, *The Singing Day*. She also leads adult community choirs, Singing in the Round, in Bath, Wiltshire and further afield. She works individually with 'non-singers' and gains tremendous satisfaction from watching people grow in confidence as they find their voice. She works with companies and institutions using singing as a tool for team-building and stress management.

For the last four years, Candy has helped coordinate a midsummer festival in Bradford on Avon with a difference: Singing Round the Town is about celebrating the spirit of the place, both the built and natural environment and the people who live there. Most of the events are participatory.

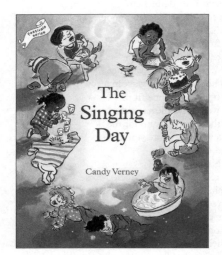

The Singing Day

Songbook and CD for singing with young children

CANDY VERNEY

'Singing can be of immense help to parents in the long haul of everyday routine,' says Candy Verney. This songbook and CD offer everything you need to turn your day into a musical, magical journey. There are traditional nursery rhymes, action games and songs, songs for waking up, getting dressed, baking and journeys.

'If doing housework with kids under your feet is a bit of a challenge, *The Singing Day* will add a joyous new dimension!'   *The Mother Magazine*

160pp; 250 x 200mm; paperback/CD
ISBN-10: 1 903458 25 0 / ISBN-13: 978-1-903458-25-9

For further information or a book catalogue, please contact:
Hawthorn Press, 1 Lansdown Lane, Stroud, Gloucestershire GL5 1BJ
Tel: (01453) 757040 Fax: (01453) 751138 E-mail: info@hawthornpress.com
Website: www.hawthornpress.com

If you have difficulties ordering Hawthorn Press books from a bookshop,
you can order direct from:
Booksource, 50 Cambuslang Road, Glasgow G32 8NB
Tel: (0845) 370 0063 Fax: (0845) 370 0064 E-mail: orders@booksource.net

or you can order online at **www.hawthornpress.com**

Dear Reader

If you wish to follow up your reading of this book, please tick the boxes below as appropriate, fill in your name and address and return to Hawthorn Press:

☐ Please send me a catalogue of other Hawthorn Press books.

☐ Please send me details of Festivals events and courses.

Questions I have about *Festivals* are:

Name _____

Address _____

_____

Postcode _____ Tel. no. _____

Please return to:

Hawthorn Press, 1 Lansdown Lane, Stroud, Gloucestershire. GL5 1BJ, UK
or Fax (01453) 751138

SY